What would Beauvoir do?

What would Beauvoir do?

How the greatest **feminists** would solve your everyday problems

Tabi Jackson Gee & Freya Rose

FIREFLY BOOKS

A FIREFLY BOOK

Published by Firefly Books Ltd. 2018

Design and layout Copyright © 2018 Octopus Publishing Group; Text Copyright © 2018 Tabi Jackson Gee & Freya Rose; Cover art and caricatures on pages 7, 8, 22, 40, 52, 70, 82, 91, 100 106, 119, 132, 143, 160, 173 © 2018 Gareth Southwell Illustration All other illustrations © 2018 Grace Helmer & Claire Huntley.

First printing

Publisher Cataloging-in-Publication Data (U.S.)

Library of Congress Control Number: 2018942045

Library and Archives Canada Cataloguing in Publication

Gee, Tabi Jackson, author
What would Beauvoir do? : how the greatest feminists would solve your everyday problems / Tabi Jackson Gee & Freya Rose.
(What would)
Includes bibliographical references and index.
ISBN 978-0-228-10133-8 (softcover)
1. Feminism--Miscellanea. 2. Feminists--Miscellanea.
3. Conduct of life--Miscellanea. I. Rose, Freya, author II. Title.
HQ1221.G42 2018   305.42   C2018-902374-0

Published in the United States by
Firefly Books (U.S.) Inc.
P.O. Box 1338, Ellicott Station
Buffalo, New York 14205

Published in Canada by
Firefly Books Ltd.
50 Staples Avenue, Unit 1
Richmond Hill, Ontario L4B 0A7

Printed and bound in China

First published by Cassell, an imprint of Octopus Publishing Group Ltd
Carmelite House, 50 Victoria Embankment, London EC4Y 0DZ

Tabi Jackson Gee and Freya Rose assert their moral right to be identified as
the authors of this work.

Publishing Director: Trevor Davies; Assistant Editor: Ellie Corbett; Editor:
Lesley Malkin; Copy Editor: Zia Mattocks; Art Director: Yasia Williams;
Designer: Ella McLean; Senior Production Manager: Peter Hunt

Contents

Introduction

Maybe you've been thinking about a pay rise. Maybe you've been thinking about orgasms. Maybe you've been wondering about what equality really means. Whatever it is, there is a feminist out there who can help you get your head around some of modern life's trickiest quandaries. *What Would de Beauvoir Do?* addresses all of these topics and more, and gives you an opportunity to explore feminist theories in detail through the lens of the questions we ask ourselves every day.

The way this book works is to ask a question as if it is coming from one specific person, for instance, "The man I'm dating insists on paying for everything. Should I let him?" or "My boss is insisting I wear high heels to work. Is this legal?" These personalized questions are used as launchpads to discuss issues that affect women from all walks of life and from around the world and, crucially, to look at how feminists past and present might have answered them.

Because the overarching question that this book tackles is not new. It's one that has been asked for centuries: should women enjoy the same rights as men? Sometimes in history this question is asked out loud, as another wave of feminism enters mainstream consciousness. But often it is something we ask quietly, to ourselves. Not just "should women enjoy the same rights as men?" but "why don't they?" and "do people treat me in the same way they would treat a man?" And "wait a minute – am I a feminist?"

Despite four waves of feminism, equal voting power (in some parts of the world) and revolutionary scientific breakthroughs like the contraceptive pill, women still seem to be dealing with the same old questions, without ever finding any satisfactory answers.

Yet feminism has continued to try to answer them. And sometimes it has even found solutions. But as the challenges changed, so did the feminist response. This means there are fascinating differences between the famous feminists – between Betty Friedan and bell hooks, between Mary Wollstonecraft and Simone de Beauvoir, between Gloria Steinem and Kate Millett.

Each of these thinkers has made a significant impact on the world we live in, and they dealt with the problems that were most pressing at the time. Surprisingly, and perhaps depressingly, all the things they fought for are still live issues in countries around the world, from trying to get the vote to being paid less than men or living in fear of male violence.

No one feminist featured in the book is more important than another, but by comparing all their ideas in the context of our own lives we can come closer to understanding what sex and gender mean, in real terms, in the modern world. To paraphrase Audre Lorde, it is in celebrating their differences that women are able to work together and find solutions. *What Would de Beauvoir Do?* is an attempt to bring all these voices and this wisdom together in one place and use it to find answers to questions that women might ask today, for instance, "What's wrong with saying that women are more compassionate than men?" "Why can't I tell my partner I'm faking it?" "Is technology sexist?" or "Why do I always feel fat?"

In this book, Shulamith Firestone's ideas on sex might change your bedroom behaviour, while Germaine Greer could make you question married life. bell hooks knows how to turn male friends into feminists, and Charlotte Hawkins Brown explains why feminism must not be seen as a white woman's game, while Rosabeth Kanter has plenty to say about ways to get more respect (and pay) at work.

Put simply, this book covers a lot of problems that women deal with in their everyday lives and tries to find solutions by looking to the huge spectrum of feminist theorists out there. From the major players that are household names to the less well-known contributors to the feminist movement – they may not agree on many things but between our panel of expert judges we hope they'll help you see the world a little differently. Think of *What Would de Beauvoir Do?* as your modern-day guidebook to feminism. Or maybe

an agony aunt – if your agony aunt was a combination of the greatest feminist minds from throughout the ages, all rolled into one phenomenal woman.

Kate Millett

7

Politics & Power

Chapter 1

What is a feminist?

Simone de Beauvoir • Olympe de Gouges • Mary Wollstonecraft • Sojourner Truth • Elizabeth Cady Stanton • Harriet Tubman • Kishida Toshiko • Francisca Diniz • Emmeline Pankhurst • Kate Millett • Rosa Luxemburg • Clara Zetkin

Women have been fighting for their rights all around the world for so long that the word "feminist" has to encompass a vast range of people with a great many ideas on what feminism and women's rights entail. It may be useful, therefore, to return to its activist beginnings and its theoretical roots, when French feminist and philosopher **Simone de Beauvoir** (1908– 86) asked, "Are there even women?" in *The Second Sex* (1949).

De Beauvoir said that it is unclear what we mean by "woman". We are told that femininity is "in jeopardy", and are urged to "Be women, stay women, become women." It seems, she says, that every female human being "must take part in this mysterious and endangered reality known as femininity". And here she lands at her point: a female "becomes" a woman through societal conditioning, which means that "she" differs from culture to culture, and can be found wanting according to the defining, prescriptive role that her society has laid out for her. "No biological, psychological or economic fate determines the figure that the human female presents in society; it is civilization as a whole that produces this creature...which is described as feminine." In laying the groundwork for a discussion of women's rights, de Beauvoir opened the door to a much less rigid understanding of womanhood, which is very much alive in the idea of gender fluidity today, and went on to pinpoint the three issues that women would come up against time and again in the fight for equality: their biological form, their supposedly "psychological traits" and

their lack of socio-economic power, since the model they are defined as being in all ways different from is "man".

Biology is not destiny

Writing in 1946, just a year after French women were given the vote, de Beauvoir declared that she had hesitated a long time before writing a book on "woman", because "the subject is irritating, especially for women, and it is not new". She may have had the Ancient Greek philosophers in mind, because way back in the 4th century BCE, Aristotle had claimed, in Book One of *Politics* (350 BCE), that women's nature and all of her potential arose from her biology. Aristotle warmed to his theme, going on to declare that "the male is by nature superior, and the female inferior; and the one rules, and the other is ruled; this principle, of necessity, extends to all mankind".

If ever there was a call for protest, this would seem to be one, but for some reason (possibly lack of economic power, political platform, collective organization and money?) women were unable to politically challenge this line of thinking for around

2,000 years – despite the fact that Sappho of Lesbos, the archaic Greek poet, had been happily ignoring the rules around women's behaviour some 200 years before Aristotle was born. On the other hand, perhaps it was precisely this tendency to wander away from doing the things men wanted them to do that resulted in the rise of cultural, economic and religious institutions around the world that would ensure that men held the reins of power in every area of life. Historian Estelle Freedman (b. 1947) has documented the ways in which networks of power around the globe evolved and gave rise to rigid class stratifications, with deep inequalities of wealth and power, especially on grounds of race and gender.

In medieval times a few lone wolves, such as the German abbess Hildegard of Bingen (1098–1179) and the French writers Christine de Pizan (1364–c.1430) and François Poullain de la Barre (1647–1723), dared to disagree with the "natural" position in which women found themselves: largely that of helpmate to a man, so he might pursue the ideal life. As the idea of "human rights" blossomed in the 18th century, other writers such as **Olympe de Gouges** (1748–93) in France and **Mary Wollstonecraft** (1759–97) in Britain (*see* page 36) began to

Suffragettes were frequently met with violence as they fought for the right to vote.

comment on the different lives of the sexes. They saw that when men spoke of "human rights", they really meant "white male rights", and they objected to this on behalf of the collective group known as "women". Feminism, as a political movement, was up and running.

Women aren't men

By the end of the 19th century first-wave feminists, such as **Sojourner Truth** (1797–1883), **Elizabeth Cady Stanton** (1815–1902) and **Harriet Tubman** (1822–1913) in the USA, **Kishida Toshiko** (1863–1901) in Japan, **Francisca Diniz** (1859–97) in Brazil

"The passivity that essentially characterizes the 'feminine' woman is a trait that develops in her earliest years [...] it is a destiny imposed on her by her teachers and by society."
Simone de Beauvoir

and **Emmeline Pankhurst** (1858–1928) in the UK, began chipping away at the accepted idea of "woman". Sojourner Truth specifically fought against the idea that "women" were white, privileged and "need to be helped into carriages", protesting in a famous speech in 1851, "I have borne 13 children, and seen them most all sold off to slavery...and *ain't I a woman?*" These first-wave feminists argued for women to be recognized as individual citizens in their own right, with full economic and political rights, but it took the collective force of women in the 20th century to coalesce the arguments into a worldwide, effective movement. These were the second-wave feminists, who took a radical stance on the world they saw around them.

Adopting de Beauvoir's *The Second Sex* as their bible, second-wave feminists started to dismantle the arguments that women's "weakness" was due to biology and psychology. They realized something else: all of the arguments were contained within a language and understanding that presumed male as Subject and woman as Other. As de Beauvoir noted, "At most [men] were willing to grant 'separate but equal status' to the *other* sex." It wasn't just the embodied power of men through institutions that was the problem; men had also organized language with "male-as-norm", according to

> ## Key consideration
>
> What are the invisible power structures that hold women back?

Australian feminist Dale Spender (b. 1943). While this seems fairly innocuous as a rule for classifying the objects and events of the world, it is actually "one of the most pervasive and pernicious rules that has been encoded," she said. It means that we grow up with the assumption that the standard or "normal human being" is a male one, and when there is just one standard, then "those who are not of it are allocated to a category of deviation". Spender says this divides humanity not into two equal parts, but into those who are "plus male" and "minus male". Women, in being different from men, are trapped into a place of insignificance and powerlessness even by the language they use.

Second-wave feminists realized that women would never gain equality or recognition unless they took a position outside of the wide-ranging male perspective. They had

> *"It is because males have had power that they have been in a position to construct the myth of male superiority and to have it accepted."*
> Dale Spender

Children have frequently had strict gender roles imposed upon them from an early age.

to look at the gender situation from the ground up, finding out what women really thought and how they lived, rather than responding to men's arguments. This decision led to the emergence of consciousness-raising groups in the 1960s in the USA and Europe. By meeting in groups and discussing their personal experiences, they were able to see collective patterns, and so begin to see how "the personal is political", as US feminists Carol Hanisch (b. 1942) and **Kate Millett** (1934–2017) suggested. As women's experience was explored from within women's own viewpoint and on their own terms, it allowed the movement to make huge theoretical leaps. Feminism has ever since moved forward through a combination of social activism and theory, with each strand informing the other.

Where Wollstonecraft had argued in the 18th century for political rights, second-wave feminists argued for a new understanding of all social, cultural and political institutions, and how they constrained women. Millett agreed with de Beauvoir that the problem lay in cultural conditioning, especially, she

said, in that it makes men develop aggressive impulses while teaching women to thwart them by turning those impulses inward. Then men mistakenly proclaim that their aggression is to do with male genitalia, not socialization, and even celebrate this by saying things like "that guy has balls", which necessarily cuts women out of the celebratory picture of competition, bravery, triumph – and power.

Socialist feminists of the second wave, such as German activists **Rosa Luxemburg** (1871–1919) and **Clara Zetkin** (1857–1933) argued that capitalism played a vital part in the oppression of women. It is only through the unpaid labour of women, such as child rearing, cooking, and caring for the sick and aged, that men are free to devote themselves to public, waged labour, they said. This sexual division of labour serves the interests of men very directly, and capitalism indirectly, in a way that pre-capitalist societies would not recognize. If women keep providing this free labour, they argued, men will keep rising through the capitalist system and maintain control of institutional power, and women will forever lock themselves out. Capitalism, the class system and women themselves need to change if the power balance was ever to shift.

Third and fourth waves

The second-wave radical feminists proved too radical for many women, and the response was a return to "femininity" with the third-wave feminists of the 1990s, who claimed there was nothing wrong in wearing lipstick and high heels, nor in dressing overtly sexually, in direct contradiction to the androgynous style adopted by their radical foremothers. Instead of fighting male dominance or cultural stereotyping directly, they took to inverting sexist, racist and classist symbols, and reclaiming words and objects previously cast aside. Third-wave feminists celebrate "difference" and see all groups and identities as equal.

It appeared as though feminism was broadening out to such an extent that the idea of men's role in the constraint of women was redundant. But then younger women, who had grown up with social media, began talking online about experiences of sexual harassment, misogyny and body shaming. As they shared their experiences, it became clear that a second round of consciousness-raising was taking place. And what emerged was a world in some ways unchanged from the 19th century: women are still being treated with disrespect (and sometimes abuse) in the workplace, the street and the home. The power dynamics remain the same. But women's ability to communicate with each other in the 21st century meant that another wave of feminism began to grow very fast. American movie producer Harvey Weinstein was one of those surprised to be knocked off his feet by this, the fourth wave of feminism.

Making a decision

So what is a feminist? American activist Gloria Steinem (b. 1934) suggested an all-encompassing definition, saying that it "is anyone who recognizes the equality and full humanity of women and men". Men are included in this invitation, because they, too, are constrained by the overarching, invisible system in which we all live, which has become known as "patriarchy". This is why Nigerian writer Chimamanda Ngozi Adichie (b. 1977) simply says, "My own definition of a feminist is a man or a woman who says, yes, there's a problem with gender as it is today and we must fix it, we must do better. All of us, women and men, must do better."

I've already got the same rights as men, haven't I?

Domitila Barrios de Chungara • Jessica Neuwirth

Women's rights are often assumed to be covered by human rights, but this is not the case. Due to their reproductive ability, they require special rights – but since these are considered too specific to be included in human rights legislature, they are often ignored and omitted. On the other hand, since women are adult humans, all human rights legislature is assumed to cover all the rights women would need. Feminists insist that gender-blind lawmaking has dangerous consequences for women, which can be explored though the field of women's rights.

During the early phases of the feminist movement, a fundamental question arose: did women want to be recognized as the same as men, or did they want to be recognized as one of two different sexes, with those differences respected by all? The danger here is that if women are the same as men, what is the problem? They simply need to work harder and break that glass ceiling. On the other hand, if women insist they are different, they are seen as a deviation from the "standard" or norm – which is male – and therefore inferior. The Brazilian feminist **Domitila Barrios de Chungara** (1937–2012) put this more directly when she addressed the first World Conference on Women held in Mexico City in 1975. She said she could see two types of liberation. One involved women who think they will only be free when they act like men and equal men in all their vices. But, she went on, "*Compañeras*, do we really want to smoke cigars?...If the man has ten mistresses, does this mean I have to do the same? What

would we be doing? We would be degrading people, nothing more."

An indigenous woman born in the Bolivian Andes, de Chungara had risen from a childhood marked by poverty and abuse to become a formidable community organizer, who staged many protests over food prices, illiteracy and inadequate medical care, before eventually running for office. De Chungara said that this wish to be like men was the path taken by "wealthy women who have everything", and it made no sense for working-class women to take the same approach. We wish to be "respected as human beings", she said, who can "solve problems and participate in everything – culture, art, literature, politics, trade-unionism – a liberation that means our opinion is respected at home and outside the home!"

De Chungara wanted real change, not intellectual acknowledgment, and she identified three key problems when it came to women's rights. First, are women's rights already enshrined within "human rights" laws? Second, if they are, is there any way of enforcing these rights? And third, are many of women's problems "at home" and therefore outside the scope of the enshrined legal rights?

De Chungara reminded her audience that in 1948 all the countries of the world created and agreed a set of human rights within the United Nations, and among these was the right of women "to participate in everything, as human beings". So we have all the rights we need, she said, in every country – including Bolivia – that signed up to the agreement. But in Bolivia, even though they say women can participate, what have the politicians done about educating, training and encouraging women to do so? Is it possible that those who make the laws do so just to persuade women to vote for a certain party, before ignoring them again?

Women have long been equated with property. In 1707, English Lord Chief Justice John Holt described the act of a man having sexual relations with another man's wife as "the highest invasion of property".

Key consideration

What would happen if women stopped fighting for their rights?

Are women's rights different?

Some feminists have argued that it is not enough for women to be recognized legally as full human beings under human rights legislation. Women's lives and daily experiences throw up different kinds of issues, which will not have been considered, including important rights to do with sovereignty over their own bodies. Religious and cultural practices have often claimed superior rights over women, especially over the use of their bodies, from practices such as FGM (female genital mutilation) to "honour killings" and being forced into marriage as a child bride (from the age of ten in some countries). A Unicef report in 2014 found that in Niger, for instance, 77 per cent of women under the age of 49 had been married before they were 18, compared to just five per cent of men in the same age group. With regards to pregnancy, every country across the world has people who vehemently argue that a man or an unborn foetus has rights that supersede a woman's rights over her own body, even from the moment of conception. A child's

The bonds of holy matrimony

right to life is included in the Convention on the Rights of the Child (UNCRC), but a woman's right to life is not included in the Convention on the Elimination of All Forms of Discrimination against Women (CEDAW).

These kinds of rights don't appear in human rights law, and if there are any laws that seem to encompass them, they are often codified by an addendum that effectively strikes them out. Algeria, for instance, signed and ratified CEDAW, but added a reservation that it should not contradict the Algerian Family Code. This had the immediate effect of striking women's rights out of the legal system within the very document that was drawn up to protect them. As **Jessica Neuwirth**, founder of the international organization Equality Now, points out, "In effect, Algeria stated its willingness to implement CEDAW so long as nothing needed to be done to implement CEDAW," just as de Chungara had witnessed in Bolivia.

Women's bodies are particularly problematic for "human rights" because of their reproductive function, which makes women susceptible to infringement of personal rights over matters to do with sex (consent and control over reproduction), entitlement to information and services for family planning, and healthcare for all issues stemming from reproduction. Pregnancy-related deaths are the leading cause of mortality for 15- to 19-year-old girls worldwide because of a lack of information and care. In Sierra Leone a

"Rights are more reliable than the kindness of someone who holds absolute power over you."
Rebecca Solnit

woman has a one-in-eight chance of dying as a result of pregnancy or childbirth, due to increased risk caused by FGM and because obstructed birth is seen as a sign of infidelity – women must "confess" to this assumed infidelity before they are allowed to access emergency healthcare.

The rights that women would like, over their own bodies and life choices, often fall into a liminal area of the law that dares not step over the family threshold, which is precisely where girls and women need protection. The 19th-century feminists who fought for the vote also demanded the right to control the terms of sex within marriage, but these were silently ignored. According to the 2011 UN report "Progress of the World's Women", only 52 countries have amended their legislation to explicitly make marital rape a criminal offence; 127 countries have not yet taken this step. Women are still fighting for public rights, such as equal pay, but also for rights that can protect them from abuse and violence within the home, from nonconsensual touch to enforced marriage or involuntary pregnancy. According to Charlotte Bunch, founder of the Center for Women's Global Leadership, New Jersey, if you add together the number of women and children in bonded labour, domestic slavery or sexual slavery today, there are more slaves in the world than at any other time in history. Slaves have no rights at all.

Making a decision:

In answer to your question, things don't look good. The number of rights you have, and their enforcement (or not) by institutions, from global corporations to police forces, depends on where you live, how wealthy you are, the colour of your skin, the health of your body and the religious belief that reigns in your environment. But women keep working to improve those rights, not just for themselves, but because "the extension of women's rights is the basic principle of all social progress", as the French politician Charles Fourier said in 1808. It seems there is much at stake, and much still to be done.

Why should I bother to vote? It won't affect my personal life.

Mary Wollstonecraft • Emmeline Pankhurst • Millicent Fawcett • Emily Davison
Elizabeth Cady Stanton • Mariya Alyokhina

The right to vote seems automatic to many women, hardly worth thinking about. In fact, many people – of all genders – find themselves feeling indifferent come election day, with no opinion about (or, perhaps, faith in) one party or another. Does it make any difference if you're a woman?

Politics often seems like a world apart, which we might comment on via social media but that goes on its own not-very-sweet way regardless of online protests or witticisms. It may feel as though the general public has always had a voice when it comes to political matters, but this is actually a relatively recent thing – for most of history and in most countries the view of the general population was deemed to be of little importance to those in power. Iceland, home of the world's oldest parliament, began to listen to the opinions of "all free men" from the year 930, and this idea of "democracy" set the tone for parliaments that followed. As they began to form across Europe, the Americas and Australasia, people of colour, women and slaves were routinely denied the right to participate in the supposedly democratic process. (In Africa and Latin America women had enjoyed near-equality prior to colonization, according to feminist historian Estelle Freedman, but lost this as European countries imposed their own systems on the invaded countries.)

Gradually things changed. Slavery was officially abolished, and by 1870 "non-white men and freed male slaves" in the USA were granted the vote. However, women had yet to be recognized as independent human beings in terms of the law, rather than objects "owned" by husbands or fathers (see pages 16–18). The official line was that women did not need the vote because it could be safely assumed that their interests would be catered for in the votes of their husbands and fathers. In addition, in most countries at this point women were viewed as being too irrational to be given the vote. They were, on the other hand, "naturally" suited to domestic affairs, which did not require a keen or intellectual mind. In 1792 writer **Mary Wollstonecraft** took issue with this idea, saying that it was wrong to view women "as if they were in a state of perpetual childhood, unable to stand alone". In her seminal work, *A Vindication of the Rights of Woman*, Wollstonecraft set out to prove that women were as intellectually capable as men, but were consistently being denied an education that would increase their knowledge and reasoning power. She also noted that there might be a political reason for denying women an education, saying, "Strengthen the female mind by enlarging it, and there will be an end to blind obedience; but, as blind obedience is ever sought for by power, tyrants and sensualists

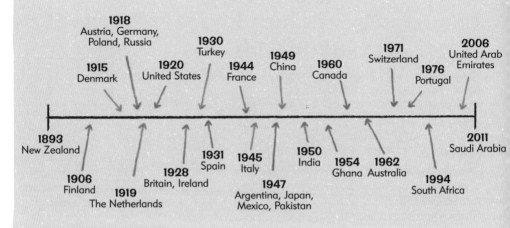

1918
Austria, Germany,
Poland, Russia

1915
Denmark

1920
United States

1930
Turkey

1944
France

1949
China

1960
Canada

1971
Switzerland

1976
Portugal

2006
United Arab
Emirates

1893
New Zealand

1906
Finland

1919
The Netherlands

1928
Britain, Ireland

1931
Spain

1945
Italy

1947
Argentina, Japan,
Mexico, Pakistan

1950
India

1954
Ghana

1962
Australia

1994
South Africa

2011
Saudi Arabia

Timeline showing the arrival of universal suffrage around the world. Countries such as South Africa, Australia and Canada gained the vote for white women much earlier than the vote for women of colour and/or indigenous women, making their universal suffrage dates much later than many on the chart.

are in the right when they endeavour to keep women in the dark, because the former only want slaves, and the latter a play-thing."

Following Wollstonecraft's lead, women began to question the fairness of locking them outside the political and legal system, and yet asking them to work within it and abide by its laws. This feeling of rumbling discontent grew and finally coalesced into the first wave of feminism during the mid-1800s (*see* page 11), when women in the UK began to organize collectively under the National Union of Women's Suffrage Societies (NUWSS). They protested in a way that was civil and acceptable: they lobbied Parliament with petitions, held public meetings and generally acted in a well-behaved manner. However, after many years of repeated failure to gain ground, including the defeat of the first women's suffrage bill in 1870, some women decided that a more action-focused, less "feminine" approach was necessary. It was time to show the entirely male government

that their campaign was serious, and that they were determined to be heard.

The bombing campaign

The new militant campaign, under the guidance of **Emmeline Pankhurst** (1858–1928) and **Millicent Fawcett** (1847–1929), saw women taking the kind of action that could no longer be ignored, such as smashing shop windows, cutting telephone wires, carving up the turf of (men-only) golf-club courses, slashing paintings of female nudes in museums, setting fire to postboxes, prominent buildings and politicians' homes, and placing bombs in St Paul's Cathedral, Westminster Abbey and near the Bank of England. In 1913 suffragette **Emily Davison** (1872–1913) was killed after trying to grab the bridle of the king's horse during the Epsom Derby horse race. She died of her injuries four days later, but her death served its intended purpose: to highlight the suffragette cause.

From 1900 to 1914 more than a thousand women were imprisoned for their actions. Many went on hunger strike and were force-fed in attempts to stop their protest. This involved tying the woman to a chair, prying open her mouth with a steel gap and jamming a rubber tube down her throat, often tearing up the throat tissue. Emmeline Pankhurst endured 12 hunger strikes in 1913, when she was repeatedly released and re-imprisoned under the Cat and Mouse Act, which allowed hunger strikers to be released until fit enough to be jailed again. On her final release in 1913, Pankhurst went to the USA on a speaking tour. "I have come to explain," she said, "what civil war is like when civil war is waged by women." At this point, the battlefield widened considerably.

The American franchise

Lucy Burns (1879–1966), Alice Paul (1885–1977) and Harriot Stanton Blatch (1856–1940) were three Americans who agreed wholeheartedly with Pankhurst that women's inability to vote meant they might forever be deprived by law of independence, through a lack of rights to inheritance, property or paid labour, and that direct action was needed.

Blatch was the daughter of one of the pioneering voices for women's suffrage in the USA, **Elizabeth Cady Stanton** (1815–1902). In 1848 Cady Stanton and fellow abolitionist Lucretia Mott (1793–1880) had held a convention at Seneca Falls, New York, to discuss the social, civil and religious rights of women. Cady Stanton gave a speech that began, "We hold these truths to be self-evident: that all men and women are created equal; that they are endowed by their Creator with certain inalienable rights." Cady Stanton pressed for voting rights constantly, and especially when a new, 15th, Amendment was to be put in place around increased suffrage. Cady Stanton and Susan B Anthony (1820–1906) argued that the new amendment should grant "universal suffrage", but those in power – all male – decided instead to insert the word "male" before "universal". Men of colour were therefore granted the vote, but American women were to wait another 50 years before they finally got the vote in 1920. By then some areas of the world had overtaken the USA in women's rights and suffrage; New Zealand granted women the vote in 1893, and by 1900 the women's movement was growing quickly around the world under the guidance of people such as Francisca Diniz (1859–97) and Bertha Lutz (1894–1976) in Latin America, Qasim Amin (1865–1908) in the Middle East, Kishida Toshiko (1863–1901) in Asia and Alexandra Kollontai (1872–1952) in Russia.

> *"The wrongs and the grievances of those people who have no power at all are apt to be absolutely ignored."*
> Emmeline Pankhurst

"Nothing strengthens the judgment and quickens the conscience like individual responsibility."

Elizabeth Cady Stanton

But I don't need to worry about all that now, do I?

Cady Stanton and Pankhurst argued that the right to vote acts to give women some say over their rights to work, wages, property and physical sovereignty (the use of their bodies), and freedom from physical attack by anyone, including their husbands. All of these battles are still being fought by women around the world today, and all of them may be challenged by each change of government. Just 22 per cent of all parliamentarians in the world are women, which means that men still control law-making around the world. And although all countries, except Vatican City, now grant women voting rights, some of those rights are heavily restricted. In Saudi Arabia women were allowed to vote for the first time in 2015, but they are still unable to access government services without a man's consent. Women in France did not gain the vote until 1944, but by 2000 they had enough influence on

government to see the adoption of a *parité* law, ensuring that candidate lists were evenly split between men and women, which has led to an increased number of women standing for election and being elected, and an equal ratio in cabinet in 2012. French feminists see this as a good starting place, but acknowledge there is still a long way to go. As Anne Hidalgo, elected the first female mayor of Paris in 2014, made clear in her victory speech: "I am the first woman mayor of Paris. I am aware of the challenge."

Key consideration

If women don't vote, and men hold all the political power, whose interests will the laws serve?

Making a decision:

According to the Inter-Parliamentary Union, the global organization of national parliaments, women's representation has stagnated globally since 2015. Women have been getting less involved in politics, rather than seeking to increase their presence in parliaments. "You have to keep acting whatever the conditions," says Pussy Riot activist **Mariya Alyokhina** (b. 1988), who was jailed for her activism. "I fight against indifference and apathy...and for freedom and choice." She invites you to join her.

Why do completely unknown men call me "sweetheart" and "honey"?

Marilyn Frye • Simone de Beauvoir • Sophie Gourion • Julia Gillard

Every female on the planet is likely to be familiar with this strange phenomenon. Its strangeness lies in the fact that a complete stranger is referring to you with an epithet that confers a false sense of intimacy, as though you already have some kind of relationship when you don't. But why is this so annoying? And why do men do that?

When complete strangers throw out apparently "affectionate" names such as "sweetheart", it produces a peculiar reaction in many girls and women. They often find themselves mentally, if not physically, recoiling, while the man is acting as though he's just being "nice" and the woman is behaving unreasonably. If she actually objects, he's fairly likely to use a put-down along the lines of "lost your sense of humour, love?", thereby injecting a second false term of endearment while apportioning all the blame for this uneasy transaction on the woman. She feels wrong-footed, whereas he goes about his business undaunted.

The American feminist **Marilyn Frye** (b. 1941) wondered about these mundane experiences and noticed that they often exert a kind of double bind. The root of the word "oppression", she pointed out in her essay "The Systemic Birdcage of Sexism" is "press", because oppression involves subjecting a group of people to various kinds of pressure in an attempt to restrict, restrain or immobilize them. Women are caught by networks of forces that expose them to penalty, loss or contempt if they break any of the rules. And the rules emanate from all sorts of forces, depending on whether a woman works outside the home or not, is on welfare or not, raises children or not, is married or not, is heterosexual, lesbian, both or neither. Pressure stems from economic status and cultural expectations (resulting from family, religion, class, or loyalties to a particular ethnic or political group) that say how "a woman should be".

In some ways this takes us back to the assertion of **Simone de Beauvoir** that women are viewed as Other by men (*see* page 12), but Frye is also interested in the particular ways that men wish women to be Other, and in the ways that men transmit these messages to women. This is the point of sexism, she says; it doesn't just deny women equality: it tells them how they should behave, and when they act in a way that oversteps the boundaries that men have drawn around "woman", they will feel a subtle pressure to get back in line.

Living in a birdcage

All the little things add up, says Frye, but they look completely harmless in isolation. Think of it like this, she says. Consider a birdcage. If you look very closely at just one of the

"Nipping at one's heels, always, is the endless pack of little things."
Marilyn Frye

wires, you could look up and down it for a very long time and not see any reason for that wire to cause a bird a problem. It would be easy to fly around it. Furthermore, even if you inspected each of the wires, one after the other, you wouldn't be able to reveal how a bird could be inhibited or harmed by it. But if you were to step back and suddenly see the whole cage, it would instantly become clear that the bird is surrounded "by a network

Marilyn Frye asks us to think of the different elements of oppression as the bars of a birdcage.

of systematically related barriers", none of which, alone, would impede flight, but taken together, confine as surely "as the solid walls of a dungeon".

This is why oppression is hard to see and recognize, Frye says, because each woman is experiencing one "wire" at a time in her daily life, while also experiencing the network of forces within which her life is lived – as a child, singleton, partner, mother, elderly woman – within her society. And the internalizing of these expectations, in the home and workplace, along with a desire to be liked – "to be good" – acts as a further reinforcement. The birdcage is made up of societal rules and expectations, both external and internalized, so that this perfect alignment seems "normal".

So what happens if a woman doesn't accept this perceived state of things as normal? What if she doesn't play the game? The first response is usually to trivialize the woman's complaint, by insisting that she's too stupid or too humourless to understand (which is often enough to cause women to roll their eyes and walk away). But there's an escalation of threat depending on the level of rebellion, according to Frye. If a woman dresses one way, it is assumed that she is advertising her sexual availability. If she dresses another way, she is said not to care about herself, or to be "unfeminine". If she uses strong language, she is a whore or a slut; if she does not, she is "ladylike" and therefore too delicately constituted to cope with robust speech or the realities of life.

False terms of endearment are useful to feminists because they allow women to get up close to one piece of "wire", says Frye, and at least look at how that particular part is operating in the system. If a woman is going about her daily business and finds herself referred to in this way, perhaps there is something inherent in the situation itself that causes a man to reassert his dominant position. It often occurs in monetary transactions, where the woman is the customer (with the power to hand over money), but it may occur in any situation in which the woman could be in danger of taking control, so there is a threat to the normal power dynamics. In 2011, when David Cameron was the Prime Minister of the UK, he tried to negate a female MP's point by saying, "Calm down, dear." In 2012, in a similar way but with a slight twist on the strategy, David Bonderman, a director of Uber, suggested that the appointment of more women on the board would result in "more talking".

These comments act to trivialize women, as "sweet little things" (objects) that need not be taken seriously. In addition, the man assumes the right to call the woman whatever he likes, for no reason other than that he feels like it, in a way that a woman would very rarely do. These terms can be used to alter the power structure within a

> ## Key consideration
> Would a man speak to another man using a similar form of endearment?

perfectly acceptable adult–adult dialogue to one involving one stronger and one weaker person, according to the now-classic article "The Pronouns of Power and Solidarity" by Roger Brown and Albert Gilman. They argue that in many languages (but lost in modern English), "you" can be said in a familiar or a more formal way, such as *tu* and *vous* in French. People understand, they said, where and when these should apply, and if both parties to a conversation address each other at the same level, they are treating each other as equals. However, if the pronouns are used non-reciprocally, they imply an unequal, hierarchical relationship. Use of a familiar pronoun (or word, such as "sweetheart") to a stranger marks a higher-ranking person speaking to a lower-ranking one, and it anticipates an acknowledgment of their greater rank by the other person replying with the more polite and formal

> *"Anything but the sunniest countenance exposes us to being perceived as mean, bitter, angry or dangerous."*
> Marilyn Frye

word. In this situation, the more familiar pronoun or word does not signal intimacy, but superiority. The woman addressed as "honey" or "dear" by an unknown man also knows (from both internalized and external societal forces) that she should be grateful. It is often a requirement upon oppressed people that we smile and be cheerful, says Frye. "If we comply, we signal our docility and our acquiescence in our situation," so the oppressive force can continue to pretend that everyone is happy with the situation. "We need not, then, be taken note of. We acquiesce in being made invisible."

However, if we don't smile, Frye suggests, we may be perceived as "mean, bitter, angry or dangerous". We may be accused of being "difficult" or unpleasant to work with, and find our jobs at risk. In the home, this unruliness has been used in courts as

justification for being physically attacked or killed, according to the journalist **Sophie Gourion** (b. 1973). She has researched the use of language used by men who have killed their partner or whole family, and found that they often put it down to a *pétage de plomb* ("blowing a fuse" or "having a meltdown") due to their partner's behaviour, rather than anything to do with themselves. She has also suggested that the media are often complicit in ignoring a long history of violence by the men in these cases. These events are not the *crimes passionnels* (crimes of passion) or *drames familiaux* (family dramas) – an expression typically used to refer to a "family annihilation" where a man murders his partner and their children before killing himself. Gourion says that these phrases act to make violence against women seem banal, normal – even trivial. "Words kill," she says.

Making a decision:

As Frye says, the choice you have to make is to smile and move on, in an invisible way, or to stand out and risk ridicule and threat. Some women have decided it is worth the fight, such as Australian Prime Minister **Julia Gillard** (b. 1961), who, in 2012, finally denounced the opposition leader, Tony Abbott, for all the bad calls he had ever made and got away with, such as his patronizing remarks about what Australian women "need to understand as they do the ironing"; or of abortion as "the easy way out". In one glorious speech, Gillard named and nailed every fallacious point and piece of sexism, one by one. So next time you're called "honey", perhaps think of Gillard, and respond in the way that she might have done.

What's wrong with saying that women are more compassionate than men?

Mary Jackman • Peter Glick • Susan Fiske • Jonah Gokova

In the long argument over whether men and women are the same or different, one of the more curious things that feminists dislike is to be stereotyped as being "nice" – being kinder, more caring, and so on, than men. At first sight these terms look like compliments, but feminists have pointed to psychological research to explain how even these "kind" ways of describing women subtly act to maintain men's position of power.

Sociologists and psychologists have explored the phenomenon of oppression across many different types of groups, and have identified ways in which an unequal relationship of power becomes entrenched. Something begins to happen over time, they noted: where there is a lot of interaction between the two groups, the intergroup attitudes may begin as purely hostile, but then they start to become ambivalent. Take any two groups in which one is dominant and one is subordinate, says American sociologist **Mary Jackman** (b. 1948) in *The Velvet Glove: Paternalism and conflict in gender, class and race relations* (1994), and watch their interactions over time. The pure hostility between them melts, because it has to – people cannot live closely together in a purely hostile way.

In colonialism, for instance, an idea developed that the white people called "the white man's burden". This allowed the white male colonialists to see themselves as good people "burdened" by the hard task of helping poor native peoples, rather than daily facing the fact that they were exploiting these peoples' bodies and lands. In this way

they were able to soothe their consciences and assuage an otherwise growing sense of guilt about their actions. In addition, in order for these myths to work as guilt-reducers, the men expressing them came to actually believe the myths were true, and convinced themselves that they experienced genuine affection for the people they were exploiting.

American psychologists **Peter Glick** and **Susan Fiske** say in their 1996 article "The Ambivalent Sexism Inventory: Differentiating

> *"The worst thing you can call a girl is a girl. The worst thing you can call a guy is a girl. Being a woman is the ultimate insult."*
> Jessica Valenti

Hostile and Benevolent Sexism" that the same kind of forces (and myths) are at work in the relationship between men and women. In hunter-gatherer societies there was no hierarchy between the sexes, but with the shift to horticultural communities, men took control over the political, economic, legal and religious institutions that grew up. Men wanted women to play particular roles that would enable the men to succeed in their own positions, and the easiest way to make women take these roles was to pretend that the women were "naturally suited" to them.

If these stereotypes are always and obviously to the detriment of the oppressed group, Glick and Fiske say, they might increase the chance of antagonism and rebellion. If, on the other hand, they are presented as *complimentary* rather than derogatory, they may more easily be accepted by the subordinate group. They may even become internalized, so that they – in this case, women – come to believe that they really do have those traits from birth. This means they are fulfilling nature's own path in supporting men in their working roles, looking after the children and home, and generally being compassionate, caring and kind.

Ambivalent sexism

The uneven power relationship between men and women has an extra element that increases the need for complimentary, or benevolent, sexist stereotyping, and that is the "dyadic power" held by women, according to Glick

and Fiske. "Dyad" refers to anything with two parts, and in any heterosexual couple there is an interdependence between two people – the men may hold the structural power, but they need women for sexual relations and producing children. Hence the ancient "joke" about women: "can't live with them, can't live without them", which dates back, via the Dutch Renaissance scholar Erasmus, to the Roman senator Cato the Elder, around 300 BCE, who said that "life with wives is uncomfortable, but without them one cannot live at all".

Unlike some groups that are hostile to one another, these two groups need each other, and what's more, they need each other in intimate ways, so they have to find a way to exist side by side, as Jackman suggests, even while the power situation continues to be unbalanced. This, say Glick and Fiske, is another reason for the blurring of hostility into ambivalence over time, which is manifested in two forms: hostile sexism and benevolent sexism. Both hostile and benevolent sexism cover three areas: paternalism, stereotyping and sexuality, but where one form is openly hostile, the other looks at first sight quite complimentary.

Hostile sexism

This type of sexism is open, no-holds-barred sexism. Glick and Fiske point to a body of research that shows it actively seeks to justify male power, traditional gender roles and men's rights to use women's bodies as sexual objects in any way they choose. Many researchers have found that in countries where women hold a much lower status than men, such as Turkey and Brazil, hostility toward women is higher (just as hostility directed toward low-caste people in India is high), and this hostility translates into a higher level of approval for husbands using physical violence to control their wives.

Men expressing hostile sexism have been found to believe that a dominating form of paternalism – keeping women in line through the use of physical strength and threats – is justified because women are weak and *ought* to be controlled by men. This approach sees women as competition (for jobs, money and so on), so they must be restricted and controlled. From this perspective, men are aggressive and dominant, and women are trying to turn the tables by controlling men. Within hostile stereotyping, women are described as bitches, hags, crones, frumps and battleaxes, among other terms. Feminists have noted that this kind of open warfare is easy to spot and to

Key consideration

Would the compliment you were given be equally flattering to a man?

stop, but the benevolent equivalent is much harder to deal with.

Benevolent sexism

The term "benevolent sexism" is applied by sociologists to describe the behaviour of men who feel affection for women and yet still feel the need to be in control within any male–female relationship, and rely on gentler justifications of male dominance and more "acceptable" stereotyping. This form of sexism looks and sounds polite.

The paternalistic approach is still there, say Glick and Fiske, but instead of being openly

Some forms of sexism are more insidious than others.

domineering, men taking the "benevolent" approach act in a more "fatherly" way. These men also consider women to be weaker, but instead of using this as an excuse to threaten them into submission, they think of themselves as protectors and providers, especially when they are in a dyadically dependent relationship, such as with wives.

Benevolent stereotypes are, likewise, less aggressive. A man taking this approach doesn't denigrate women so much as idealize them, researchers have found; they tend to place women on a pedestal, rather than throw them in the gutter. These men see women as calm, compassionate, nurturing, caring, sweet and all the other attributes that might make for the perfect wife and mother. As if by perfect coincidence, these caring women and those domestic roles are the perfect fit. Everything about the benevolent sexist view is therefore justified as "natural", and in this way, it becomes incontestable. Men who take the benevolent approach are most likely to describe their wives as "my better half", say

Glick and Fiske. In terms of sexuality, these men do not use women's bodies as objects to treat in any way they wish; they view them as objects that will make them "complete", in an apparently romantic way.

So is there any hope? In his well-known speech "Challenging Men to Reject Gender Stereotypes", given in Zimbabe in 1998, feminist **Jonah Gokova** (b. 1956) suggests a way out of this two-streamed, no-win situation. Men should change their attitude toward sex, he says, and realize how much they themselves are losing under patriarchy, such as the right to express their feelings openly, even in front of women, as there are proven links between the need to totally suppress emotion and high levels of stress or even heart attacks. Gokova aligns with de Beauvoir when he says that within patriarchy men are having to "project an image that is not naturally theirs – and this is not sustainable". Living the "myth of male superiority" is hurting men and women, he claims, and men need to change.

Making a decision:

If you feel strange about a compliment, you may have experienced benevolent sexism. It sounds polite, but it situates you in an inferior position in the power dynamic. Similarly, describing women as "more compassionate" than men is shorthand for insisting that women have more access to their emotions. Since rationality is valued more highly than emotional intelligence in most contemporary societies, this acts to propel men into a more superior position.

Is feminism just a white woman's thing?

Charlotte Hawkins Brown • Adrienne Rich • Bettina Aptheker • Kimberlé Crenshaw • bell hooks • Angela Davis • Combahee River Collective

In 1920 African-American suffragist and educator **Charlotte Hawkins Brown** (1883–1961) told a conference of white women about her train ride to the venue in Memphis. She spoke of how a dozen white men had forcibly removed her from the sleeping car and dragged her into the segregated "blacks only" day coach. Angry and humiliated, Hawkins Brown told the audience, "The thing that grieved me most is that there were women in the car and there wasn't a dissenting voice."

Hawkins Brown, who was to become co-founder, with Mary McLeod Bethune (1875–1955), of the National Council of Negro Women, asked the white women in the audience to consider what it must have been like to have been her, in that situation. "Just be coloured for a few minutes," she said. She went on to tell her audience something of how it was to be black in the USA in the 1920s; of the terrors of lynching and rape, and the daily assaults and insults that black women were forced to bear. Hawkins Brown was trying to force white women to think outside of their own experience and reconceptualize their idea of "woman", to realize that the white woman's experience and theories had been particular to them, that they had been white-centric and they had not been all-encompassing.

In 1989 white Jewish-American author **Adrienne Rich** (1929–2012) again tried to help white women make the shift that Hawkins Brown had suggested: to see outside and beyond their own privilege. Even when we switch on the TV "news" in the USA, Rich said in "Notes Toward a Politics of Location", it is "telling the citizens of my country [that communism] is on the move in Central America, that freedom is imperilled, that the suffering peasants of Latin America must be stopped". Rich argues that this extremely narrow perspective of the world keeps white people locked into a discourse that positions all non-white people as inferior, and prevents white people from seeing and exploring difference. It prevents them from being able to imagine being "coloured" even "for a few minutes".

> *"It is not our differences that divide us. It is our inability to recognize, accept, and celebrate those differences."*
> Audre Lorde

Defined through embodiment

We must look at the politics of identity location, Rich said. Each of us is located in one particular body, which "even from the outset...had more than one identity". From the very start, "I was viewed and treated as female, but also viewed and treated as white". Rich recognizes that in being located in a body, it means "more than understanding what it has meant to me to have a vulva and clitoris and uterus and breasts. It means recognizing this white skin, the places it has taken me, the places it has not let me go."

This is true of all men and women, and all types of physical characteristics. They affect people's reactions to us and deliver us a particular experience of the world. Rich explained that the second-wave feminists (*see* page 12) had been "trying to see from the centre", to ask questions about women from a woman's point of view, rather than a man's. We wanted to create a society without domination, she says; "the problem was that we did not know whom we meant when we said '*we*'." White women, she said, must come to terms with their whiteness, and realize that although they have been marginalized as women, they must realize that they "also marginalize others, because [their] lived experience is thoughtlessly white".

In 1989 socialist feminist **Bettina Aptheker** (b. 1944) said in *Tapestries of life: women's work, women's consciousness, and the meaning of daily experience* that if white women sincerely wish to understand the experience and oppression of women of colour, they need to "pivot the centre". This

means working to centre another person's (or group's) experience as the main perspective, while at the same time maintaining the recognition of your own position, so that both people, or groups, are held in a position of value and attempt a real understanding of perspectives. In her 1994 article "Women, Ethnicity and Empowerment", Nira Yuval-Davis quotes professor Elsa Barkley Brown as saying, "All people can learn to center in another experience, validate it, and judge it by its own standards without need of comparison or need to adopt that framework as their own."

Intersectionality and difference

Kimberlé Crenshaw (b. 1959), professor of Law and civil rights advocate, introduced the term *intersectionality*, also in 1989, to explain how the experience of black women is that of being oppressed by several forces at the same time. In her groundbreaking article, "Demarginalizing the Intersection of Race and Sex", Crenshaw invites us to imagine a traffic intersection where many roads meet, and traffic may flow in any direction. If an accident happens, it may have been caused by a car or cars coming from any or all of these roads or directions. Likewise, a black woman may be harmed by sex, race or class discrimination, or all of these at once, because she may live at the centre of these intersections.

Crenshaw showed that black women are discriminated against in ways that do not fit into the legal categories of racism or sexism, and often find themselves unprotected in law by either of these categories. For instance, during the 1964 court case known as DeGraffenreid versus General Motors, five black women failed to win their case of illegal dismissal. They were found to have been dismissed on the basis of "last in, first out", rather than anything to do with discrimination. They clearly had not been dismissed because they were black, the judge said, as black men still worked at the factory. And they clearly had not been dismissed because they were women, because white women still worked at the factory. As Crenshaw pointed out, the order of hiring people into the factory over the years had been white men, black men, white women, black women. It was as a result of being both black *and* female that led to the black women being in the most precarious position. However, the court ruled that while "the plaintiffs are clearly entitled to a remedy if they have been discriminated against", there could be no "super-remedy" that combined the two forms of discrimination.

Key consideration

Can a wealthy white person understand the lived experience of a poor – or wealthy – woman of colour?

Finding themselves at the intersection of race and class discrimination meant that black women "fell through the cracks" in terms of the law.

The African-American activist **bell hooks** (b. 1952) has pointed out that interlocking political systems lie at the heart of America's and Europe's politics, which came together during the 19th century to create a perfect storm of "imperialist, white-supremacist capitalist patriarchy". White supremacy assumes that white-skinned people are superior to others, hooks says, and they are

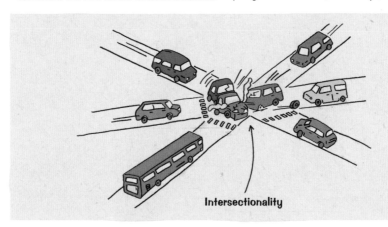

Intersectionality

likewise "imperialist" in assuming they have a right to exploit the resources and people of colonized countries – which included the assault and rape of black women by white masters/owners, as activist **Angela Davis** (b. 1944) has demonstrated. Capitalism is an economic system that favours those who own the means of production, and hooks defines patriarchy as "a political-social system that insists that males are inherently dominating, superior...and endowed with the right to dominate and rule". Working-class women and women of colour, the world over, are affected by both of these intersecting forces in a way that middle- and upper-class white women are unaware. Worse still, hooks suggests, white women have not been anxious to call attention to race and class privilege because they have benefited from them, as many wealthy white women have counted upon "there being a lower class of exploited, subordinated women to do the dirty work they were refusing to do".

From intersectionality to identity politics

In recent times intersectionality has led to the burgeoning of identity politics, which has not only recognized difference, but has increasingly led to groups refusing to work with one another – preferring instead to organize and protest individually. In turn, this has recently led to cases of feminists being denied a platform to speak in universities and other public spaces. Iranian feminist and human rights activist Maryam Namazie (b. 1966) is one among many feminists who are concerned about this censorship. She pointed out on the Feminist Current podcast in 2016 that freedom of expression is, for some women, the only freedom they have to dissent and resist – and that feminists are working across the world to diminish the feminization of poverty and violence against women. Women should be fighting together, Namazie says, supporting one another and working together under the larger political goals of equality and human rights.

Making a decision:

In 1977, a black feminist lesbian organization in the USA known as the **Combahee River Collective** issued a famous "Statement". In this they said that the feminist task is "the development of integrated analysis and practice based on the fact that the major systems of oppression are interlocking". If feminists are to improve the lives of all women, they need to continually "pivot the centre" to listen to all women, and locate and protest against every force ranged against them.

Why doesn't feminism ever get us equality?

Susan Faludi • Mary Wollstonecraft • Barbara Santee

This is a great question, because United Nations studies show that nowhere in the world have women achieved socio-economic and political equality to men, despite four "waves" of feminism (*see* page 14). And yet a 2017 poll by Ipsos across 23 countries found that 45 per cent of women already think they have achieved full equality. So what's going on?

The United Nations Development Programme (UNDP) Gender Inequality Index of 2017, using information gathered from 23 countries, shows that 72 per cent of men in the USA think women have equal opportunities, as do 76 per cent of men in India and Canada, and 67 per cent of men in the UK. Not surprisingly, perhaps, fewer women (around 45 per cent) surveyed said that they thought they had equality. That said, both men and women hold views that distort reality. The American author **Susan Faludi** (b. 1959) researched the discrepancy in the early 1990s and realized that this distortion was part of a phenomenon that has ultimately caused each wave of feminism to fail. She called this "backlash".

Taking the term as the title for her 1991 book, *Backlash: The Undeclared War against American Women*, Faludi set out to explore in detail how every gain made by feminism is very soon undermined by its opponents in society, especially through the use of the media. And the most common tool for flipping back years of gain is the same each time, she says. It is the idea that feminism has harmed women, and so feminism itself is the source of all women's problems,

not inequality or the patriarchy. Faludi found countless examples of headlines proclaiming that professional women were suffering from "burnout" and early heart attacks, while also becoming victims of an "infertility epidemic". Single women were said to be grieving about a "man shortage", and becoming "depressed and confused" about their situation. These cries were everywhere, Faludi said – at the newsstand, on TV, in movies, in advertisements, and even in academic journals and doctors' offices. Unwed women were "hysterical" said *The New York Times*; they were crumbling under "a profound crisis of confidence". It's enough to make a sane person shout, "Stop! Whatever is causing this nightmare must be found and made to cease immediately!" Which, of course, is exactly the effect they were tailored to produce – because that "thing" was feminism.

Whores and emasculators

The first major book of feminist theory to be published in the West, in 1792, was *A Vindication of the Rights of Woman* by **Mary Wollstonecraft**. Wollstonecraft is considered by some to be the founder of

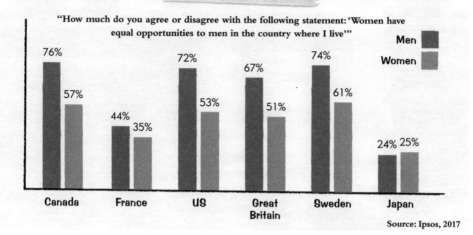

"How much do you agree or disagree with the following statement: 'Women have equal opportunities to men in the country where I live'"

Men
Women

	Canada	France	US	Great Britain	Sweden	Japan
Men	76%	44%	72%	67%	74%	24%
Women	57%	35%	53%	51%	61%	25%

Source: Ipsos, 2017

feminism because, as the English author Virginia Woolf (1882–1941) said, "We hear her voice and trace her influence even now among the living." And yet for a century after her stirring call to action against the lack of education and financial independence available to girls and women, Wollstonecraft's name was almost irredeemably smeared. She fought, she said, not for women to "have power over men, but over themselves". It does not sound like a radical idea, but in fact it prefigures by 67 years the "classic" principle developed by British philosopher and economist John Stuart Mill (1806–73): "Over himself, over his own body and mind, the individual is sovereign." While Mill's version would be fêted by philosophers from its publication in his 1859 essay "On Liberty"

onward, Wollstonecraft's version − spelling out women's right to have power over themselves − was greeted with a mixture of confusion, agreement and hostility.

By the time she died at the age of 38, Wollstonecraft's ideas had been roundly trounced in the press and by the intellectuals of the day. She herself, they also noted loudly, was a disgrace: she had given birth to an illegitimate child, and then set off across the world to catch up with a Norwegian captain to whom she had taken a shine, writing a bestselling book along the way. Her biography, written by her husband William Goldwin and published after her death, unwittingly revealed what a free-thinking woman she really was and, as a result, Wollstonecraft (along with her ideas)

"The anti-feminism backlash has been set off not by women's achievement of full equality but by the increased possibility that they might win it."
Susan Faludi

was dismissed as a "poor maniac" and an unnatural being: a "hyena in petticoats". Her early death – in childbirth – was no more or less than she deserved, they said.

Victorian backlash

Wollstonecraft was ultimately dismissed with such public disgust that even her most avid readers were persuaded to drop her ideas. The backlash against her early feminist arguments was to reach its full potential in the British Empire of the Victorian era, when white male supremacy, institutionalized misogyny and overt sexual prudery (alongside private sexual violence) became the order of the day. The dominant ideology (or norm) for middle- and upper-class women was purity, piety and domesticity (also called the "cult of true womanhood"). Women were expected to take a passive stance toward life, while applauding the achievements of their husbands and fathers as they enriched themselves through "undiscovered" resources from around the globe. Modern feminists note that backlash arguments against feminism continue to move around these same terms of sexuality, exploitation, misogyny and the idea of man's "natural" supremacy.

Fortunately for the fate of womankind, the suffragettes objected to this state of affairs, and took up the campaign for legal rights and representation for women. A few, such as American campaigners Voltairine de Cleyre (1866–1912) and Margaret Sanger (1879–1966), were also active in campaigning for women's sexual and reproductive rights. All

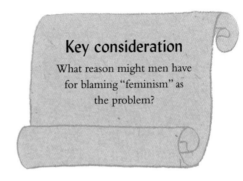

Key consideration

What reason might men have for blaming "feminism" as the problem?

these women and groups were denounced as "hysterical" and "mad", and as greedy old hags who wanted to take everything from that long-suffering creature, man. One postcard from the time shows a poem called "This is the House that Man Built", which describes women who want the vote as "the sly Suffragette, who is all on the get, and wants all, in the house that Man built". The suffragettes' struggle for equality was reframed as a grab for men's power, so they were shown as wearing men's clothes and doing "men's jobs". Since men had power over women at the time, so male reasoning went, the suffragettes were really looking to reverse the situation, so that women would "be in charge" in the home and the workplace. This idea – that women are seeking power over men, not equality – has been used as a constant counter-argument to feminism in every backlash ever since the 1900s.

A forced return to domesticity

The second-wave feminism of the 1960s and 1970s (*see* page 12) disrupted the idea of the 1950s housewife in the Western world, so the backlash inevitably included the cry that the feminists were destroying women's "natural" talents as homemakers and parents. Feminists were trying to do away with femininity itself, the papers screamed (which was true, in a way), and replace it with an androgynous look that was unattractive. The 1970s and 1980s saw women and men wearing more androgynous clothes, with both sexes wearing makeup, if they felt like it. Women began to gain ground in the workplace and enter some of the most male-staffed institutions. The ensuing backlash, according to Faludi, centred on widespread myths of the "barren womb", man shortages and depressed singletons, which she found to be a distortion of the facts. As Faludi notes in her book *Backlash*, the message was this: "You may be free and equal now but you have never been more miserable." Feminism has done this to you but, luckily, there are (expensive) ways we (the fashion, dieting and cosmetic industries) can make you gorgeous and feminine again. "We are told time and again," according to Faludi, that "the women's movement…has proved women's own worst enemy."

Today, with a new rise in feminism and the momentum of the powerful campaign against rape and sexual harassment that began in India in 2012, and picked up momentum via the USA in 2017, some feminists feel that another backlash is inevitable. By December 2017 the Twitter feeds were alive with tweets that suggested things had perhaps already "gone too far", which was exactly the suggestion that kickstarted the 1980s' backlash, according to Faludi.

Making a decision:

Every new wave of feminism has been met with the claim that it is feminism itself that is responsible for women's woes. The American activist **Dr Barbara Santee** (b. 1937) says, in her 2012 "Letter to a Young Activist: Do Not Drop the Banner", that the way around this is simple. When the suffragists stood in front of the White House in 1917, demanding the vote, they were arrested and dragged off by the police. Before being taken away, each one passed her banner to another suffragist. The women changed, but the banners remained. Just as it took women 70 years to win the vote, Santee says, we must make the same commitment to equality now – we must keep on picking up the banner.

Dating & Relationships

Chapter 2

The man I'm dating insists on paying for everything. Should I let him?

Simone de Beauvoir • Kate Millett • Gloria Steinem

Dating may be a relatively modern phenomenon but it has still formed its own unique set of gender-based "rules". Even now, it is usual for men to expect to have to pay, and for women to expect them to do so. In 2017, Match.com's annual "Singles in America" survey found that although 47 per cent of women said they would offer to pay the bill because they wanted to show their independence, a further 74 per cent said they did it so they didn't feel any obligation to do anything with their date.

What obligations are we talking about here? Traditional dating guidelines included the man's obligation to pay for the date and the woman's obligation to withhold sex and to offer it as a gift to the man she loves. These systems developed at a time when women were less likely to work and were economically disadvantaged compared to men, and they set an awkward precedent for what men and women expect from each other on a date. This has not translated well into modern life and has given feminists plenty to talk about: never are you fulfilling your role in a patriarchal, capitalist society as much as when you are on a heterosexual date in a global restaurant chain with a man paying the bill.

The first-wave feminists (*see* page 11) did not directly try to solve this very prevalent modern issue; "dating" has only really been occurring since the 1920s. Prior to that a man and a woman would never go out in public together unwed, unless in the presence of a chaperone – let alone dine in a restaurant or frequent a local bar for a few Margaritas.

When women were without work or access to cash, there was never a question of who paid for whom: it was the man who took the woman out. The man did the asking, so the man did the paying. Prior to that, partnerships would be set up by families, so a man and woman's courtship took place in a woman's home with her extended family present.

Now, it is most likely that you have chosen your prospective date yourself, or at least accepted his invitation for courtship without familial influence. And you probably have money of your own, so you don't *need* a man to pay for you. This complicates things.

One thing that has not changed is that the economics are still stacked against you. For as

"Far too many people are looking for the right person, instead of trying to be the right person."
Gloria Steinem

long as men and women have been courting, men have typically earned more money than women. And in a capitalist world, money is power. Even in the situation where your date is earning less money than you, the gender roles, which you have learned from society, your parents and the vast amount of media at your fingertips, are all working against you both.

Key consideration

Am I a bad feminist for letting a man pay for a date?

Is chivalry dead?

Let's start with the expectation that the man has to pay. Each time a feminist movement has attempted to define what it means to be a woman, they have done so in the context of what it means to be a man. In the second volume of her 1949 book *The Second Sex* **Simone de Beauvoir** (1908–86) opens with one of her most famous lines: "One is not born, but rather becomes, a woman," and, following her suit, the second-wave feminists (*see* page 12) explored

how people of both sexes learned gender and the roles they were expected to play. In the instance of a date, your partner has not decided in a vacuum that it is he who must foot the bill. Rather, literature, movies, television, advertising and history have taught him that this is what he should do.

So if you are earning more than him, does this still make sense? Probably not. In which case it becomes a case of benevolent sexism (*see* page 30). Benevolent sexism can be defined as any chivalrous behaviour toward women (or men) that feels favourable but is actually sexist because it fulfils stereotypes, and in this case puts the woman in a position of weakness.

Transactional relationships

In its crudest terms, if a man pays for all your dates and you, in turn, repay him by having sex with him, this sets up the foundations for a transactional relationship. The man is buying you. This, feminists would argue, is problematic, particularly when set against the backdrop of sex work and how the economics of that operate.

To revisit Match.com's "Singles in America" survey, let's recall the second statistic: that 74 per cent of women offered to pay something toward the bill so they did not feel obliged to do anything with their date. So the question remains: are you offering to pay because you want to, or because you are worried your date will expect something from you in return for his payment?

Further studies have looked at sexual behaviour on dates and found that on one American campus 83 per cent of women had encountered male sexual aggression on dates since their senior year of high school. What is more, feminist ideology and the sharing of dating expenses have not shown to be linked to fewer reports of offences on dates. By that reasoning, splitting the bill will not save you from sexual aggression, but choosing the right partner hopefully will.

The new rules

Radical American feminist **Kate Millett** (1934–2017) encouraged readers of her formative work, *Sexual Politics* (1970) to dismantle the gender stereotypes that trap both men and women. Millett spoke of "instrumental" masculinity and "passive" femininity. Reiterating the common theme of power imbalances in heterosexual interactions and relationships, Millett argued that the roles we adopt do not just restrict us, but encourage us into behaviour patterns that we ourselves are not even comfortable with. American feminist **Gloria Steinem** (b. 1934) championed the need for women to wake up to their whole beings, and not to be afraid to do things differently. According to Steinem's self-esteem-focused brand of feminism, rather than judge if your partner is right for you by his actions, consider your own actions first.

Making a decision:

Your date is not doing any visible harm by paying for you, but he is carrying on a long line of tradition that used to involve men using money and power as influence. A sensible guideline could be to presume that whoever asks for the date pays for it, but in order for that to work equally, you would need to initiate the same number of dates as your partner. "Far too many people are looking for the right person, instead of trying to be the right person," said Steinem. Be bold, in other words. Dare to offer to pay for a date, and see if your partner is offended or not. You might learn something about him – and yourself.

Can I use online dating apps without objectifying myself?

Naomi Wolf • Shulamith Firestone

Online dating is no longer a peripheral pastime for young people looking for easy "hook-ups". Studies have found that online dating is the fastest-growing means for unmarried couples to meet. Swiping right for love is an activity that has become a part of our culture. But do all these image-based quests for love just make us objectify the human body more?

Dating applications and websites largely work on a visual premise. To use them you must upload images of yourself, and tell prospective partners details about yourself in a profile. In putting pictures of yourself on the internet and asking strangers to "like" or "swipe right" on them, to find a match, you are seeking validation (based almost entirely on your looks) from external sources.

It is no wonder you feel objectified. But at the same time, are you not also objectifying men? Online dating is a two-way street and, in many ways, the shallowness of judging someone on their looks is simply a method of searching efficiently through thousands of people to find a partner. It is a numbers game after all. Or that is what the applications would have you believe, at least.

When the second wave of feminists was debating censorship, nudity and the female body during the sexual revolution in the 1960s, they did not have dating applications to consider. However, they were thinking about how women are presented and how they present themselves at a time when image-based communication was exploding amid the rise of television and full-colour magazines. *Playboy* was first published

in 1953; and by the 1970s pornographic material was rife.

It is a fact of modern life that on any image-based communication platform, you are going to be judged on your looks. Add to that the relative anonymity of using a dating website and you have some peculiar and unprecedented territory. While a number of websites work hard to ban obscene photographs and prevent aggressive behaviour, many people have reported not feeling safe when using them.

Levelling the playing field?

For good or bad, another side-effect of dating apps is to level the playing field slightly. Women are now encouraged to judge men on their looks, too. In *The Beauty Myth* (1990) American author **Naomi Wolf** (b. 1962) examines how this shift might affect society (pre-dating apps, of course). "The fact is that women are able to view men just as men view women, as subjects for sexual and aesthetic evaluation; we too are effortlessly able to choose the male 'ideal' from a lineup; and if we could have male beauty as well as everything else, most of us would not say no," says Wolf. "But so what? Given all that,

> *"Women everywhere rush to squeeze into the glass slipper, forcing and mutilating their bodies [...]. But they have no choice. If they don't the penalties are enormous: their social legitimacy is at stake."*
> Shulamith Firestone

women make the choice, by and large, to take men as human beings first."

Dating apps encourage an aesthetic-based selection process, where no one takes the opposite (or the same) sex as "human beings first". According to researchers, this is having an unprecedented effect on men's wellbeing. One study shows that men who regularly use the app Tinder have more body-image concerns and lower self-esteem. Users reported lower levels of satisfaction with their faces and higher levels of shame about their bodies. What is more, users were also more likely to view their bodies as sexual objects.

Wolf's argument reminds us that while men may be subjected to this now, there is still an imbalance. Men are expected to objectify women from an early age, whereas women are not expected to objectify men. "If girls never experienced sexual violence; if a girl's only window on male sexuality were a stream of easily available, well-lit, cheap images of boys slightly older than herself, in their late teens, smiling encouragingly and revealing cuddly erect penises the color of roses or mocha, she might well look at, masturbate to, and, as an adult, 'need' beauty pornography based on the bodies of men."

It is possible for men to reject this training, says Wolf. "If both genders were given the choice of seeing the other as a combination of sexual object and human being, both would recognize that fulfilment lies in excluding neither term." This behaviour is not encouraged on many dating websites.

The rise of "ghosting" (where users stop talking to someone out of nowhere) and "negging" (where one user takes down another's self-esteem by making negative remarks) suggests that the opposite is happening, and that these platforms are encouraging worse human behaviour rather than better.

Is love racist?

The power of dating apps on the societies that use them cannot be understated. While on one hand they are altering how people find mates, on the other there are studies suggesting that they are increasingly dictating, what we find attractive in potential partners.

Between 2009 and 2014 the dating app OKCupid analysed the interactions of many of its users (the number involved in the survey altogether amounted to 25 million people). The study found that compared to black, Asian or minority ethnic users, white users got more messages. White users were also found to be less likely to reply to or match with users of a different race from themselves. So the chances of making a successful match (if measured against the chances of getting a response) were, simply, higher if you were white.

So are dating apps racist? Not exactly, it is just that their users are clearly skewed toward a certain (white) look. And while this study looks at only race, it stands to reason that this is not the only societal problem being exacerbated by technology. If men and women are looking for the mainstream "ideal" and hoping to appeal to the most people possible (remember, dating apps are a numbers game) individuality is not being celebrated but, rather, ironed out.

> ## Key consideration
> Are dating apps levelling the playing field between men and women?

This is the homogeneity of love. The Canadian-American feminist **Shulamith Firestone** (1945–2012) lamented on the patriarchy's blanket ideals in *The Dialectics of Sex* (1970), arguing that in order to get along in the world, women were being told they must look a certain way. "Women everywhere rush to squeeze into the glass slipper, forcing and mutilating their bodies with diets and beauty programmes, clothes and makeup, anything to become the punk prince's dream girl," she says. "But they have no choice. If they don't the penalties are enormous: their social legitimacy is at stake."

When translated into the modern world of online dating, one thing is clear. The world has not evolved to be more accepting of our differences but, rather, less so. If you don't conform to society's ideals, then you are less likely to find love. You must be a clone

"If both genders were given the choice of seeing the other as a combination of sexual object and human being, both would recognize that fulfilment lies in excluding neither term."
Naomi Wolf

to increase your social currency on dating platforms. "Thus women become more and more look-alike," says Firestone. "But at the same time they are expected to express their individuality through their physical appearance." It is a no-win situation.

Unsolicited "dick pics"

Then there is the other modern phenomenon forced into our consciousness in the wake of the rise of dating apps: the "dick pic". According to market research firm YouGov, 53 per cent of millennial women have received one, and one in four millennial men have sent one. The psychoanalytically minded feminists would have a field day with this.

Penises were a great preoccupation of the Austrian founder of psychoanalysis Sigmund Freud (1856–1939) in his understanding of human psychology, particularly in his development of the *"penis envy"* theory. To put some complicated theory very crudely, the penis was a source of power, Freud argued. You can see why men would want to show theirs off. In a broader sense, feminists argued that males interpret women's desire for status and equality as an effort to castrate men. The penis has a lot to answer for.

For a very long time, men could have many sexual partners while women could not. Therefore, only men could compare their experiences. Then, in the 1960s, the sexual revolution happened and women could share their own experiences – discussing their partner's performance, comparing penis size and so on. While the jury is still out on whether men and women discuss such matters in equal measure, one thing is for sure: the unsolicited dick pic is simultaneously an attempt to prove male prowess and a display of sexual power.

Making a decision:

Many sites now attempt to prevent this sort of behaviour and some go even further and try to disrupt gender stereotypes, like Bumble for example, where women make the first move. The "feminist" dating platform encourages new behaviours that challenge its users, both male and female. While objectification may be an unavoidable side-effect of using an image-based platform, it does not mean that dating apps cannot also uproot the power balance in modern courtship. Or, as Shulamith Firestone would have it, alter our narrow ideas of what love looks like.

What's wrong with one-night stands?

Carole Vance • Gloria Steinem • Shulamith Firestone • Mary Daly

Women have fought long and hard for sexual liberation. And yet "sleeping around" is still looked upon negatively, particularly if it is a woman doing it. "Slut shaming" is a regular practice in the media and there is a pronounced double standard in how society treats men with many sexual partners as opposed to how it treats women. So what is going on here?

At the dawn of the 1970s the sex life of women was becoming a hot topic. Some feminists were fighting ferociously for women's rights to exercise their sexual desires, while others were arguing that as long as we live in a patriarchal society, women's sexual desires will never truly be satisfied.

While the "one-night stand" is a modern phenomenon, women being branded as "sluts" or "whores" for wanting to have sex is not. In the UK and USA before birth control and sexual liberation in the 1960s, the only women really prepared to take the risk of extra-marital pregnancy were sex workers, for whom it was a financial imperative. The next time you get called a "slut" for sleeping with someone, remember that name may have more historical baggage than you realize.

The double standards exercised between the sexes here is another hot topic for feminist theory. In Britain, back in 1862, a committee was established to inquire into venereal disease in the armed forces. On its recommendation the first Contagious Diseases Act was passed. The legislation permitted police officers to arrest women suspected of being prostitutes in certain ports and army towns. The women were then subjected to compulsory checks for sexually transmitted diseases. If a woman was declared to be infected, she would be confined in hospital.

These measures were taken to protect men in the army from disease. Because military men were often unmarried and

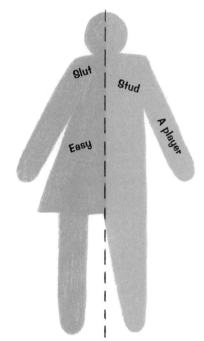

Double standards are rife in the language we use about male and female sexuality.

> *"The sexually aggressive or even expressive woman may be a slut or even a nymphomaniac, but the sexually aggressive man may be normal or even admired."*
> Gloria Steinem

homosexuality was a crime, prostitution was considered a necessary evil. No one proposed to subject the men to such checks and confinement, however, and it was on this basis that an angry debate began over inequality. This early political issue prompted one of the first occasions that women organized themselves and actively campaigned for their rights.

Pro-sex feminism

From the right to earn money through any means necessary to the right to sleep with whomever you want, these sorts of battles are still raging today (albeit more quietly). To say there is something wrong with how you want to exercise your sexual freedom is distinctly antifeminist. Modern feminism is founded on your power to choose; and the rise of the sex-positive movement in the 1970s spoke directly to this – sexual liberation was advocated as an expression of sexual power and pleasure. Hence the parallel campaign for LGBT (lesbian, gay, bisexual and transgender) rights: sexual liberation meant loving whomever you wanted to love and expressing yourself in any way you wanted to, whether through a heterosexual relationship or not.

Going by the name of pro-sex feminism, sex-radical feminism or sexually liberal feminism, the men and women who adopted these schools of thought would be very much on side with your decision to sleep with the people you wanted to sleep with. Sexual freedom is an essential component of your human rights. And anyway, sex between two consenting adults is not for anyone else to judge.

Sex-positive feminists opposed legal or social efforts to control sexual activities between consenting adults. Famous sex-positive feminists include the American writers Carol Queen (b. 1958) and Susie Bright (b. 1958) – also known as Susie Sexpert – whom the *Los Angeles Times* once dubbed a "feminist bad girl". "Her credo is simple: Sex is fun. Prudery kills," reads the piece from 1994. "Fantasies are healthy and important. And given empathy, latex and some basic instruction, anything that occurs between two consenting adults is A-OK."

"F" is for

FUN!

Susie Sexpert's rise to fame came at a troubled time for people of all sexualities in America, the article goes on to acknowledge: "Between AIDS, Christian chastity clubs, anti-porn campaigns and date rape controversies, the national libido seems to be in full retreat. The time was ripe for someone with a librarian's knowledge, a mother's concern and a hooker's candor to put the F-word, *fun*, back into sex."

Key consideration

Why are men called "studs" and women called "sluts"?

Patriarchy in the bedroom

Radical feminists in the 1980s and 1990s, such as Andrea Dworkin (1946–2005) and Catharine MacKinnon (b. 1946), were in opposition to the pro-sex movement in what became known as the Sex Wars. They would tell you that more often than not, when having sex, you are merely taking part in a man's own pursuit of ecstasy. Dworkin and MacKinnon's school of thought argued that as long as women continue to live in fear of rape and sexual abuse, they will never have sexual freedom.

These women might not say there is anything wrong with you having one-night stands, but they would want you to protect yourself from this sort of aggression. Under the radical feminism of the 1970s, your sexuality cannot be fulfilled until greater

safety is established. American feminist **Carole Vance** explored the nuances of this idea in her 1984 book, *Pleasure and Danger: Toward a Politics of Sexuality*:

"The tension between sexual danger and sexual pleasure is a powerful one in women's lives. Sexuality is simultaneously a domain of restriction, repression, and danger as well as a domain of exploration, pleasure, and agency. To focus only on pleasure and gratification ignores the patriarchal structure in which women act, yet to speak only of sexual violence and oppression ignores women's experience with sexual agency and choice and unwittingly increases the sexual terror and despair in which women live."

Gloria Steinem also got in on this argument. Women are often seen as mere objects in sex, she argued. You are not able

"Sexuality is simultaneously a domain of restriction, repression, and danger as well as a domain of exploration, pleasure, and agency."
Carol Vance

"A revolutionary in every bedroom cannot fail to shake up the status quo."

Shulamith Firestone

to be in control of your own sex life because of the way we understand sex as a society. "Even the words we are given to express our feelings are suffused with the same assumptions," says Steinem in her 1983 book *Outrageous Acts of Everyday Rebellion*. "Sexual phrases are the most common synonyms for conquering and humiliation (being had, being screwed, getting fucked); the sexually aggressive or even expressive woman may be a slut or even a nymphomaniac, but the sexually aggressive man may be normal or even admired."

The limitations of the sexual revolution

Radical feminist **Shulamith Firestone** had great hopes for the sexual revolution and the freedom it would give women. But before that, a lot would need to change. "The socialist-feminist revolution will free both women and children, leaving them with complete economic independence and sexual freedom, and integrating them fully into the larger world," was her expressed hope.

Firestone also suggested that men were unable to love women without degrading them. This is why the "sexual revolution" has not meant liberation for women, she said. Because women are still bound by the double standard and the need to combine love and sexuality.

American philosopher **Mary Daly** (1928– 2010) took an unusually spiritual approach to this problem, recommending that women's sexuality and the ideal of chastity was simply another tool of oppression used by misogynists and the patriarchy. Daly would have you consider your sexuality and spirituality in the same breath, seeing sex as not simply a human function but an ecstatic, otherworldly one, too.

Making a decision:

The crux of the argument for extreme feminists is this: as long as women reproduce, they will not have sexual freedom – that is, the freedom and pleasure that these feminists hoped contraception and the sexual revolution would provide. Your ability to create human life is what is holding you back (sorry). Looks like we're still waiting for the revolution to happen, then.

Why can't I tell my partner I'm faking it?

Anne Koedt • Germaine Greer • Simone de Beauvoir • John Stoltenberg • Betty Friedan

---

When it comes to women's sexuality, there is much that the world does not know. Studies have found that women find it harder to orgasm than men and they also find it harder to say what works for them in bed. Is this what is happening with your partner? Is this a feminist issue? And if so, what can you do about it?

The female orgasm is a biological mystery and it is also a cultural one. It has remained something of an enigma, thanks to being largely ignored and in many cases even censored out of literature, movies and the media. But this is about you, not the media. Or is it?

If you are struggling to climax, you are most definitely not alone. Research conducted by the condom brand Durex in the Netherlands (published as "The Orgasm Gap") shows that almost 75 per cent of women in the Netherlands and Belgium do not orgasm during sex, whereas only 28 per cent of men say they don't always climax. Durex calls this "orgasm inequality". It also found that lesbians have more orgasms than heterosexual women, so this affliction is more specific to women in straight relationships than any other group.

There are many reasons why feminists believe women feel the need to fake orgasms, and a lot of them have to do with, well, being a woman. Maybe you don't want to hurt your boyfriend's feelings. Maybe you feel like it is your fault. Maybe you are worried you will topple him off his masculine perch if you admit that you have never orgasmed and have been faking it all along. Maybe you just think it is the easy way out. Whichever it is, you are probably doing yourself and your boyfriend an injustice by pretending. But it may not all be your fault.

The myth of the vaginal orgasm

One of the greatest mysteries surrounding the female orgasm is: why does it exist in the first place? It serves no purpose in the exact act of reproduction (men can have sex with women and produce babies with the woman experiencing no enjoyment at all). Scientists have still not found an answer to this question.

Some people even go as far as doubting the very existence of the female orgasm. Feminists – and women full stop – have been fighting this misconception for a long time, and the importance of this battle cannot be underestimated. There are still cultures around the world where female pleasure is a sin, hence the horrific practice of female genital mutilation (FGM). This, many feminists would argue, is one of the main reasons why we still need feminism today.

The first scientific study of women's sexuality was undertaken by American

research team Masters and Johnson, who published their findings in a book, *Human Sexual Response*, in 1966. Two years later **Anne Koedt** (b. 1941) wrote an essay on women's sexuality, looking at the findings of Masters and Johnson from a radical feminist perspective. This essay was called *The Myth of the Female Orgasm* and it looked at evidence for the clitoral orgasm, female anatomy and reasons why the "myth" of the vaginal orgasm was (and still is) maintained.

Koedt explored how Sigmund Freud (1856–1939) and his approach to women's sexuality, or their lack of it, had reinforced misconceptions borne in the Victorian era about things such as hysterical behaviour and the notion that women were inferior to men. But she also considered whether his idea that women learn to be frigid as a natural

reaction to men's dominance may have some truth in it. Perhaps women and men are both afraid of female sexuality? It was these sorts of topics that Koedt was not afraid to tackle and, in doing so, she set a new precedent for what could and could not be discussed in the public sphere.

Are women simply frigid?

If you are "faking it" to your boyfriend, then clearly you belong in the group of people who do believe in the female orgasm. So what is going wrong? Australian-British writer **Germaine Greer** (b. 1939) laments in her 1970 book *The Female Eunuch* that the reason women are so unfamiliar with their own sexual needs is because, from a young age, unlike boys, they are encouraged not to understand themselves. "The little girl is

> *"Pornography tells lies about women.*
> *But pornography tells the truth about men."*
> John Stoltenberg

55

not encouraged to explore her own genitals or to identify the tissues of which they are composed, or to understand the mechanism of lubrication and erection. The very idea is distasteful."

Simone de Beauvoir (1908–86), who was remarkably ahead of her time in talking about female sexuality, took this comparison between men and women and used it to initiate a debate about the politics of sex. In *The Second Sex* (1949), she proposed that if a man has the desire to have sex, he will have sex, climax and then no longer have the need for it. For women, this progression does not appear to be so linear, or so simple.

The chances are, if you are finding it hard to orgasm, it could well be due to lack of experience and not knowing yourself well enough. As much as the female orgasm has been ignored, it has also been underestimated. How can you understand something so complicated if you are taught it is supposed to be easy?

Are the media to blame?

We see examples of this over and over again in the media. You and your partner have both seen movies and TV shows where women come at exactly the same time as their male counterpart, with zero foreplay and straight, penetrative sex. If women are learning from movies, books and porn that women can come like that, the next step is to suspect that if you can't, there must be something wrong with you. You learn to improvise to avoid failing to fulfil your own and your partner's expectations. You learn to lie.

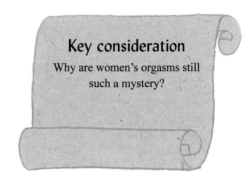

Key consideration

Why are women's orgasms still such a mystery?

As radical American feminist **John Stoltenberg** (b. 1944) said: "Pornography tells lies about women. But pornography tells the truth about men." In the 1989 romantic comedy *When Harry Met Sally*, Meg Ryan's character famously tries to debunk some of these lies when she demonstrates how easily she can fake an orgasm, attempting to persuade Harry that he may not be the sexual impresario he thinks he is. "It's just that all men are sure it never happens to them and most women at one time or another have done it," quips Sally. "So you do the math."

The feminine mystique

During the so-called Sex Wars of the 1970s, feminism focused a great deal on sex, pornography and censorship. In her 1963 book *The Feminine Mystique* **Betty Friedan** (1921–2006) used popular psychology of the time to try to understand women and their sexuality. She argued that in the absence of agency and exploration, women "evade human growth" and "will never know sexual fulfilment and the peak experience of

> *"It's just that all men are sure it never happens to them and most women at one time or another have done it, so you do the math."*
> Sally, *When Harry Met Sally*

human love until they are allowed and encouraged to grow to their full strength as human beings".

Friedan quotes a 1930s study by psychology professor Abraham Maslow (1908–70) where the relationship between sexuality and "dominance feeling" or "self-esteem" or "ego level" in women was examined. Contrary to what you are often shown on TV and in movies, the research found that the more dominant the woman, the greater her enjoyment of sex and the more easily she orgasmed. These women were more themselves, Friedan noted, and therefore they could give themselves to love.

But in reality this does not happen often, says Friedan. During a woman's first sexual experience she understands that she is there to facilitate the male orgasm. She is playing a part in a fantasy where the woman must be submissive and please her partner, as she does in everyday life.

YES, YES, YES!

Perhaps the most famous fake orgasm ever? Meg Ryan in *When Harry Met Sally*.

Making a decision:

Friedan and her contemporaries argued that only a woman who is able to express herself in everyday life can reach orgasm and thus take a leading role in her own (sex) life: "The transcendence of self, in sexual orgasm, as in creative experience, can only be attained by one who is himself, or herself, complete, by one who has realized his or her own identity," she wrote. The female orgasm does exist. And your right to orgasm is a woman's right. A human right. Seize it.

I'm happy and successful. Who cares if I have a partner?

Germaine Greer • Shulamith Firestone • bell hooks • Gloria Steinem

Your job is going swimmingly and you are enjoying life. Yet every time you are at a social gathering – or worse, visiting your extended family – all anyone wants to know is if you are dating anyone. And if you are not, why not. When will these regular intrusions into your personal life end? Should you say yes just to shut them up? Why do you even care what they think?

Cast your mind back to just a hundred-odd years ago, when a single woman would be without a vote and unable to do much on her own. That should not make you feel bad about your relationship status – quite the opposite – but consider it a bit of helpful context when it comes to understanding why so many of your friends and relatives are interested in your love life. Not so long ago, a woman could quite literally not function in the world without a man. Looks like some people are still catching up.

The "single" woman is a modern phenomenon – and you will have noticed she gets a lot of airtime. Whether it is newspaper articles telling you your time is running out to procreate or your best friends suggesting that you try another new dating app, we live in a world where the solo female is at odds with the status quo.

Hence the labels: if you enjoy sex, you are a whore; if you don't want to marry, you are a spinster; if you practise self-love, then you are most likely a witch. These labels have been developed for you because you are trying to live outside the traditional man's world, the *patriarchy*. Women are for making babies, so

without a man to help you secure the future of the human population, what exactly is your purpose?

Spinster versus bachelor

A single man in your position is not asked these sorts of questions, as many feminists have pointed out. In *The Female Eunuch* Australian-British feminist **Germaine Greer**, who was one of the most prominent thinkers of the second wave of feminism (*see* page 12), digs down into this double standard: "The woman who remains unmarried must have missed her chance... the man somehow never found the right girl." During the second wave of feminism many women were preoccupied with the difference between what men were allowed to do in regards to personal relations and what women were allowed to do. Here, Greer provides a clear illustration of the differences in how society treats two people in the same position, just because of their sex. "In the common imagination nuns are all women disappointed in love, and career-women are compensating for their failure to find the deepest happiness afforded mankind

<blockquote>
"In a male-run society that defines women as an inferior and parasitical class, a woman who does not achieve male approval in some form is doomed."
Shulamith Firestone
</blockquote>

in his vale of tears." In Greer's vision of a patriarchal society, you being single is either a sign of disappointment in love or of personal failure. Take your pick.

Patriarchy and capitalism

Another woman who rose to prominence during the second wave of feminism was Canadian-American **Shulamith Firestone**. Firestone's approach was radical and she paid particular attention to the work of socialists Frederick Engels (1820–95) and Karl Marx (1818–83). Through adopting their manner of political thinking she investigated the suppression of the lower classes and women, and used these parallels to explain how women were oppressed under the systems of patriarchy and capitalism. What has this got to do with your relationship status? Well, quite a lot actually.

"In a male-run society that defines women as an inferior and parasitical class, a woman who does not achieve male approval in some form is doomed," reflects Firestone in her 1970 book *The Dialectics of Sex*. "To legitimate her existence, a woman must be more than woman, she must continually search for an out from her inferior definition;

and men are the only ones in a position to bestow on her this state of grace." Firestone would no doubt applaud you on your strength and determination in the face of people who expect you to settle down and meet someone. Whether you like it or not, Firestone observed, your identity is so tied up with the opposite sex that you are only allowed to love yourself if a man loves you first.

Key consideration

Why does a single woman who exists outside a patriarchal family unit worry people so much?

Loving yourself first

As you would expect from thinkers and activists who cut their teeth in the 1960s and 1970s, in an age of antiwar protests and sexual liberation, the second-wave feminists had a preoccupation with self-love and self-actualization. If you feel like you are missing something from your life, they would suggest it is self-love, not a man.

This starting point of self-worth and

self-respect, many second-wave feminists believed, was what was needed to change society and change how women viewed themselves. "When we can see ourselves as we truly are and accept ourselves, we build the necessary foundation for self-love," said American feminist **bell hooks** (b. 1952) in her 2000 book *All About Love*. "Giving ourselves love we provide our inner being with the opportunity to have the unconditional love we may have always longed to receive from someone else."

Another feminist with an interest in love and its relationship to self-esteem is **Gloria Steinem**. By her own approach to feminism, the American writer would encourage you to focus on the effect of those outward pressures on your sense of self-esteem, and how your personal life is dictated by society and what it expects from you.

Steinem's advocation of self-love is reminiscent of more modern approaches to social issues. She urged women to look for love in themselves before looking for it in other people. She called women searching for love "addicts" and suggested they were

Steinem advises us to learn to love ourselves before trying to love other people.

> *"In the common imagination nuns are all women disappointed in love, and career-women are compensating for their failure to find the deepest happiness afforded mankind in his vale of tears."*
> Germaine Greer

looking for themselves in the wrong place, in a "foreign substance". In her 1993 book *Revolution from Within* she wrote, "Like other addicts, many of us are still in denial: we still believe we can find the rest of ourselves in a foreign substance; that is, in the body and mind of another person."

According to hooks and Steinem, if you can battle past this sexist ground where your friends and family only think you have achieved something if you have managed to catch a man, and find a place of self-worth away from the male gaze, you could then come to a deeper understanding of yourself.

Making a decision:

Whichever way you look at it, these leading feminists would have you remember that life is more than just a waiting game. You can be happy and unhappy both with or without a man. Steinem wrote from the heart about this in *Revolution from Within*: "Fortunately, feminism came along to help me and millions of others try to become ourselves, with or without marriage, to understand, in the brilliant phrase of some anonymous feminist, that we could 'become the men we wanted to marry'." Maybe your relatives just care about your happiness. And maybe it is hard being surrounded by lots of other people in relationships all the time. But if you are happy and you are being true to yourself, that is a rebellion in itself. As Steinem says: the revolution comes from within.

Can my boyfriend be a feminist?

Robert Jensen • John Stuart Mill • John Stoltenberg • bell hooks

Just because someone has a penis it doesn't mean they can't be a feminist, too. Gender stereotypes imprison all of us. Does your boyfriend feel under pressure to be "manly"? Do you wish he would get past his protein-shake phase and stop trying to look like the Hulk? All through history there have been many male allies to the feminist cause, who have seen how both men and women can benefit from breaking down society's expectations of them.

Ask your boyfriend what living up to male stereotypes has ever done for him. Fulfilling gender stereotypes is something feminists have been asking women not to do out of obligation for centuries, and the same applies to men. For instance, it is "manly" not to talk about your feelings; it is "manly" not to be caring; it is "manly" not to respect women. And it is "manly" to watch porn and laugh about it with the guys afterward. Boys will be boys, as the dangerous cliché goes.

And this really is dangerous. Numerous studies have shown that men with strict ideas about masculinity are more likely to be aggressive toward women. In the same way as there is pressure on women to behave in a certain way, there is also a similar pressure on men. Feminism can't by nature address one without changing the other.

There are, of course, some men who believe that masculinity and power are interlinked: these men are called supremacists. They love the patriarchy because it puts them in control and they would never identify as feminists because feminism seeks to disrupt the very systems that benefit them.

This leads us on to the darker side of how these gender roles manifest themselves in traditional relationships. We are taught that there is a power inequality between men and women – so much so that the expression "she wears the trousers" is still bandied around, as though one party has to be dominant and the other submissive. More often than not, though, the "dominant" role is expected to be occupied by the man.

It is not such a stretch to see how this leads to violence against women and even a rape culture. Research consistently shows that

There is no one way to be a feminist.

men who perpetuate traditional gender roles are more likely to have a history of sexually coercive behaviours, are more likely to blame the victims of rape and are more accepting of intimate partner violence. Second-wave feminists (*see* page 12) argued strongly and convincingly that women would never be safe, particularly in bed, while men continued to exhibit this behaviour toward women.

Why feminism is good for your relationship

In contrast, a study found that women in relationships with men who identify as feminists had healthier relationships, both in terms of quality and long-term stability, than those in relationships with non-feminist men. Perhaps you could present this argument to your boyfriend, along with an explanation of how feminism is actually not just for the benefit of women, but for everyone.

One question that may then arise is: can a man even be a feminist? The term "Men in Feminism" was first used in an edited anthology of that name by Alice Jardine and Paul Smith in 1987. In this instance, men were separated into two groups. In the first group were those who acknowledge the systems that benefit them, but also argue that not all men are oppressors. In the second group were those who explore what it means to be a man and the practices and discourses that shape masculinity in various social, cultural and historical contexts.

But how does this relate to everyday life? Someone who has recently argued for the case of male feminists is American professor of journalism **Robert Jensen** (b. 1958). In his 2017 book *The End of Patriarchy: Radical Feminism for Men* Jensen presents the ways in which men can be allies and agents of change without trying to "rescue" women (and once again fall into the trap of being the ones in power). Jensen describes feminism as a gift for men, and says it is the most compelling way to understand sex, gender and culture. He also shows how the patriarchal rules that govern all of us are harming humans and the planet we live on (incidentally, many famous feminist thinkers have also been environmental activists).

Great male feminists

The history of men in feminism is a long and complicated one. One of the first significant male contributors to the fight for women's rights was British philosopher and political economist **John Stuart Mill** (1806–73).

"If we do not work to create a mass-based movement which offers feminist education to everyone, females and males, feminist theory and practice will always be undermined by the negative information produced in most mainstream media."
bell hooks

Together with his wife Harriet Taylor Mill (1807–58), a prominent early women's rights activist, he penned an essay in 1861 called *The Subjection of Women*. In it they wrote: "[T]he principle which regulates the existing social relations between the two sexes – the legal subordination of one sex to the other – is wrong in itself, and now one of the chief hindrances to human improvement; and that it ought to be replaced by a principle of perfect equality, admitting no power or privilege on the one side, nor disability on the other."

A more recent male representative of the movement is **John Stoltenberg**, who was at one point married to the prolific feminist

Key consideration

What male stereotypes are holding your boyfriend back?

thinker Andrea Dworkin (*see* page 182). Stoltenberg founded the group Men Can Stop Rape in 1987, but he is probably best known for his theoretical writing, especially his 1989 book *Refusing to Be a Man*. In it he argues that there is a necessity for men to take the responsibility of creating a less toxic version of masculinity, which is based on respect, rather than misogyny.

Feminism is for everybody

This is all tied up with a buzzword that has shaped the 21st-century feminist movement: intersectionality (*see* page 33). The origins of this idea can be traced back to the likes of African-American feminist **bell hooks**, who helped save feminism from becoming an academic institution and attempted to mould it into a movement that benefited everyone, from the working classes to minority ethnic groups, not just the privileged who had

FEMINISTS

Men can, and should, be feminists.

"Without male allies in struggle, the feminist movement will not progress."
bell hooks

> *"[T]he principle which regulates the existing social relations between the two sexes [...] is wrong in itself, and now one of the chief hindrances to human improvement; and that it ought to be replaced by a principle of perfect equality..."*
> John Stuart Mill & Harriet Taylor Mill

the time to write about it. In her book *Feminism is for Everybody*, published in 2000, she writes: "Feminism is a movement to end sexism, sexist exploitation and oppression." Essentially, the problem isn't men: the problem is sexism, so hooks embraces feminist men. "Without male allies in struggle," she writes, "the feminist movement will not progress."

hooks looks at how the patriarchy negatively affects men as well as women, encouraging them to suppress their emotions and teaching them they should be dominant and all-powerful. So ultimately, says hooks, men need a feminist education as much as women. "Men often tell me they have no idea what it is feminists want," she says in

Feminism is for Everybody. "I believe them." She continues, "If we do not work to create a mass-based movement which offers feminist education to everyone, females and males, feminist theory and practice will always be undermined by the negative information produced in most mainstream media."

Recent arguments for "why men should be feminists" have encouraged men to enter the fray for their mothers, wives and daughters. This cheapens the argument, feminists have argued. Feminism should be taken up because women are fellow human beings, not because they are family members.

Making a decision:

So in short: yes, your boyfriend can be a feminist and there are countless reasons why he should be one, too. But he doesn't have to quit playing football and swap beer for Prosecco. Feminism wants people not to be obliged to do what society expects of them because of their sex, but it doesn't mean they can't take part in activities that mirror those norms. (Unless they are behaviours such as misogyny and sexism, which serve no good purpose whatsoever.)

I want to propose to my boyfriend. Can I?

Shulamith Firestone • Simone de Beauvoir • Germaine Greer • Judith Butler

Marriage proposals are a curious thing. Chances are you both know you are going to get married at some point. You may have even discussed how many children you are going to have, where you are going to live and so on. Maybe you live together already. Maybe you already have a child. Yet no matter how many modern and egalitarian steps you have taken together as boyfriend and girlfriend, it remains your boyfriend's "job" to propose, and yours to sit around waiting for him to ask.

Despite the boxes you have already ticked off, attitudes toward marriage proposals have not changed much. Some studies even suggest they are going backward. While three-quarters of Americans say it would be fine for the woman to do the proposing, in theory, the same study shows that young adults are more likely than their elders to consider it "unacceptable" for a woman to do the asking.

Regardless of the progress of women's rights, sexual liberation, reproduction and so on, proposals are stuck in a microcosm of tradition. Even the fundamental ideas behind it are out of date, such as the practice of asking the woman's father for her hand, which is historically based on her being treated like a piece of property. As for the notion that the engagement ring should cost two months' salary? That can be traced back to a very effective advertising campaign by diamond jewellers De Beers in the 1930s.

So how has it survived in its dusty, yesteryear form? And why – even though you are in an equal partnership – do you feel like you can't propose to your boyfriend?

Love is simple. Relationships aren't

In her 1970 book *The Dialectic of Sex: The Case for Feminist Revolution* **Shulamith Firestone** investigated how power plays out in relationships between men and women, and how that same power alters our personal feelings. For Firestone, love is simple but it is relationships that present problems. Love "becomes complicated, corrupted, or obstructed by an unequal balance of power," she says. "We have seen that love demands a mutual vulnerability or it turns destructive: the destructive effects of love occur only in a context of inequality."

By Firestone's reckoning, the thing that make you feel strange about proposing is that it would require you to acknowledge the power balance in your relationship. That is, for historical and questionable reasons, men do the asking, women do the responding.

Heterosexual engagements are the only ones in which this question is an issue. In the USA, in two-thirds of states, gay marriage is now legal; men propose to men, and women propose to women, and yet, in a male-female relationship there remains this hearty hangover of tradition.

From the proposal to the white dress, to the bride's father walking her down the aisle and her parents having to foot the wedding bill, everything about marriage is a minefield of rituals that feminists have taken aim at as preserving the rules of capitalism and the patriarchy. If you look under the microscope at these traditions, as Firestone and her contemporaries did, things start to become destabilized. This, Firestone explains, is because, "Women and love are underpinnings. Examine them and you threaten the very structure of culture."

Two months' salary

Why men propose

In the past (and in some cultures still) a woman's marriage would be arranged for her, so the discussion as to who would propose was redundant. A young woman would be passed from her maternal home to a new domestic life, along with a dowry, if available, and would become her husband's property.

In her 1949 book *The Second Sex* **Simone de Beauvoir** considers what happens when a man and a woman have sex, and it is not far from the loss of autonomy that women often experienced (and to some extent still do) in marriage. "He projects himself towards the other without losing his autonomy; feminine flesh is a prey for him and he seizes in woman the attributes his sensuality requires of any object…It is he – as for most animals – who has the aggressive role, and she who submits to his embrace." Man captures woman. Man proposes to woman. Man does, woman submits.

Another study in 2011 by S Sassler and A Miller, "Waiting To Be Asked: Gender, Power, and Relationship Progression among Cohabiting Couples," looked in depth at a group of working-class couples in America in an attempt to understand what roles gender and power played in their relationships. Although these women and men challenged

"We have seen that love demands a mutual vulnerability or it turns destructive: the destructive effects of love occur only in a context of inequality."
Shulamith Firestone

how gender is performed, cohabiting men remained privileged in determining relationship progression. "The findings suggest that adherence to conventional gender practices, even among those residing in informal unions, perpetuates women's secondary position in intimate relationships." In further details of the survey, some men even suggested it would be laughable if a woman proposed to them. Similarly, many of the women deemed it absurd that they would propose to their boyfriends, despite them often determining the relationship in other more pragmatic ways – for instance, the boyfriend moving in and them splitting their rent. So do we hold on to this tradition because we like it? While tradition isn't always a good thing, it does hold significant weight in our culture and emotional lives.

In the same study researchers thought they may find a correlation to the challenging of gender norms. While a few norms were flipped, the researchers found the men were still given the "outcome power" because their partners interpreted the male proposal "as an expression of love and caring". From "destination proposals" (think the Eiffel Tower and beaches) to other overblown romantic gestures, this is the one time men are expected to unveil their softer, romantic, more "feminine" side and show in no uncertain terms how they feel.

> ## Key consideration
> Can you ever have an equal partnership if you don't feel like you could propose to your boyfriend?

Germaine Greer is typically cynical about such gestures, suggesting they mask the absence of something else and are little more than smoke and mirrors. "Women are hypnotized by the successful man who appears to master his fate; they long to give their responsibility for themselves into the keeping of one who can administer it in their best interests," she says in her 1970 book *The Female Eunuch*. "Such creatures do not exist, but very young women in the astigmatism of sexual fantasy are apt to recognize them where they do not exist. Opening car doors, manoeuvring headwaiters, choosing gifts, and earning money, are often valued as romantic attainments: in search of romance many women gladly sacrifice their own moral judgement of their champion."

> *"It is he – as for most animals – who has the aggressive role, and she who submits to his embrace."*
> Simone de Beauvoir

Greer argues that women want the romance *because* it is make-believe – they will happily suspend their own rational thoughts in order to abandon themselves to a world where men are their saviour and marriage their place of safekeeping. Therefore, proposing to a man simply does not work for the woman who wants to believe in the fairy tale. It involves you having agency and self-determination, and taking your fate into your own hands.

The performance of proposal

Being the "master" of your destiny sounds like something a man would do, of course, not a woman. And here we enter more problematic territory. Would it make you

look too aggressive, too independent, or too headstrong, if you were to propose to your partner?

American philosopher **Judith Butler** (b. 1956) did a great deal of work looking at gender constructs. In her seminal 1990 book *Gender Trouble: Feminism and the Subversion of Identity* she develops Simone de Beauvoir's idea that "one is not born a woman: one becomes one" and argues that a "becoming woman" can also be seen as a performance. Women are encouraged or even forced to uphold feminine traits and behaviours. This may explain your own hesitation to propose – it defies the very identity that you have inherited as a woman from the patriarchy.

Making a decision:

Getting engaged without the man doing the asking, even in the 21st century, is a big deal, as you have already acknowledged, but what does it say about your prescribed gender roles? He can't be man, provider and upholder of the patriarchy unless you are mild, obliging and his subordinate. Just as it takes strength against adversity for a woman to propose to a man, it takes a man who is sure of himself and your relationship to accept that proposal.

Marriage & Domestic Life

Chapter 3

Fairy-tale wedding, fairy-tale marriage?

Mary Wollstonecraft • Simone de Beauvoir • Roxane Gay • Marilyn Friedman

According to much of modern media, films, and literature, marriage is a moment of finality and resolution for women, and the beginning of a life of imprisonment for men. And in many countries marriage really is the only way that women can control their future. In the absence of education and financial independence, it is often the only route out of poverty.

In most developed countries, however, marriage is not a financial imperative, particularly among those who are privileged and educated. And yet marriage rates remain high. People still choose the institution regardless of how many choices and opportunities they have available to them.

What this institution looks like to you depends on not only where you live in the world, but also what religion you follow (if any), what your family and friends have done before you, and what cultural and economic influences you experience. Yet regardless of what your own fairy-tale wedding looks like, it is likely to involve a big celebration with lots of friends. So how has this longstanding institution continued to be popular in so many cultures and religions?

Why is marriage so important?

When writing her witty book on the ups and downs of modern marriage, *Wedding Toasts I'll Never Give* (2017), Ada Calhoun asked rabbis and priests why they thought people get married. According to them, most couples, when asked, could not answer. One priest described this as a "cultural crisis". Can you and your partner answer this question?

Don't feel bad if you can't; a quick spin back through feminist history will show you that it is a question women have battled with for hundreds of years. **Mary Wollstonecraft** (1759–97), one of the founding figures of the women's rights movement, explored the way that marriage was seen as a right to the wrongs of mankind, and an opportunity to improve the relations between men and women. In her 1792 book *A Vindication*

> *"The wedding is the chief ceremony of the middle-class mythology, and it functions as the official entrée of the spouses to their middle-class status"*
> Germaine Greer

of the Rights of Women, she wrote, "It is acknowledged that they spend many of the first years of their lives in acquiring a smattering of accomplishments; meanwhile, strength of body and mind are sacrificed to libertine notions of beauty, to the desire of establishing themselves – the only way women can rise in the world – by marriage." But marriage was not a solution to anything, she reasoned. Human nature is human nature, and no big, white wedding will change that.

Do we prioritize marriage over love?

This is a question that **Simone de Beauvoir** (1908–86) addressed in detail in *The Second Sex*. Like many other feminists who followed her, she thought that women often lose sight of love and instead focus on society's expectation of them to be married.

Perhaps this is because in many religions a man and a woman are not recognized as partners until they have been married in the eyes of their god or gods. Perhaps it is because historically women couldn't operate in society without a man (they could not vote, and going somewhere on your own was at best frowned upon and at worst dangerous).

So are we still experiencing a hangover of this today? De Beauvoir suspected so. Thanks to social conditioning, marriage is the answer, not just love: "She no longer embellishes her future spouse with a prestigious halo: what

she wishes for is to have a stable position in this world and to begin to lead her life as a woman." In de Beauvoir's eyes, women find themselves wanting to marry in order to gain status, not necessarily to find love.

And so, we lose sight of reality by believing in a happy ending. What comes after has little significance, as long as you find "the one". How many Disney films show a middle aged couple having marital problems they need to overcome? The happy ending is the end of the story. It's the goal.

Encouraged by these stories of romance and Prince Charmings, some girls even plan their perfect day years before meeting a man they wish to marry. (Although it is worth noting that the "happily ever after" ending is a relatively modern addition to some of these ancient tales.)

The fairy-tale wedding: spend, spend, spend

Weddings are not cheap. According to the *The Knot* website, the national average cost of a wedding day in the USA in 2016 was $35,329, an increase of as much as $2,688 from the 2015 average of $32,641. In most parts of the world now, from South Korea to rural France to North America, weddings revolve around spending money – lots of it.

If the bridal magazines are to be believed, this is because the size of your engagement ring and the cost of your wedding are in direct correlation with how successful your marriage will be. Yet one study found the exact opposite to be true. In "'A Diamond is Forever' and Other Fairy Tales: The Relationship between Wedding Expenses and Marriage Duration", Andrew Francis-Tan and Hugo Mialon surveyed 3,000 married people in the USA and concluded that more expensive weddings did not equal happier marriages.

Key consideration

Do big weddings distract people from the lifelong relationship that comes after it?

It isn't just the magazines that sell you this dream. From children's literature to advertising to movies, we are taught to believe that marriage somehow makes life better. This "salvation" is exploited by brands purveying the myth of romantic love and marriage: big expensive gestures are how you tell someone you love them, right? From car manufacturers to jewellery businesses, these companies attach their wares to narratives of romance and love to encourage men and women (but mostly women) that more things will equal a better life.

American feminist **Roxane Gay** (b. 1974) explores how material things are connected to modern love in her 2014 collection of essays titled *Bad Feminist*. In particular she looks at the extraordinary amount of product placement in the modern-day fairy tale that is E L James's *Fifty Shades of Grey* (2011). In one entry titled "The

Trouble with Prince Charming, or He Who Trespassed against Us", Gay quips: "If you have a materialistic fantasy, this book will curb that edge."

Anastasia Steele and her knight in shining armour, Christian Grey, venture into a world (E L James's version) of BDSM (bondage and discipline, dominance and submission and sadomasochism) in what has been dubbed "mummy porn". But when the clichés and orgasms are finished, even this dysfunctional modern couple get their happily ever after. "My amusement with *Fifty Shades of Grey* only goes so far," laments Gay, after indulging her readers in some light-hearted observations. "The books are, essentially, a detailed primer for how to successfully engage in a controlling, abusive relationship." This is quite a price to pay.

"...strength of body and mind are sacrificed to libertine notions of beauty, to the desire of establishing themselves — the only way women can rise in the world — by marriage."
Mary Wollstonecraft

So what is a girl to do?

The biggest price you pay in marriage, though, as American philosopher **Marilyn Friedman** (b. 1945) would tell you, is losing your independence. In most cultures, regardless of where you are in the world, a bride is property to be transferred to her new husband's family.

In Russia the ceremony often involves the groom paying a ransom to buy this new property – a *vykup nevesty*. In China the bride is likely to be presented to the groom's family in a traditional red wedding carriage. And in most traditional Christian weddings she will be walked down the aisle and "given away" by her father.

In her 2003 book *Autonomy, Gender, Politics*, Friedman argues that for this reason marriage is more dangerous to women than men: because women are seen to bring less to a relationship than their male counterpart. The woman is taken, or transferred, to her

Women have historically been viewed as property to be passed from family to family.

new family. In extreme terms, your husband provides for you, he gives you security, he is the rescuer. He is your Prince Charming. Or not, as the case may be.

Making a decision:

As Gay points out – as did de Beauvoir before her, and Wollstonecraft many years before that – women are taught from childhood that marriage is some kind of great escape. A ceremony that you work toward having with a loved one, after which you will leave your old life behind for something shinier, newer and better. The dream of the fairy-tale wedding, the late, great feminists would say, is an illusion that brides-to-be are encouraged to buy into, in order to forget that they are giving up their own lives for a life of domestic servitude and looking after their husbands. And so…they lived happily ever after.

Should I take my partner's name after marriage?

Barbara Smith Bodichon • Kate Millett • Betty Friedan

Changing your name when you marry your partner is still a common cultural practice across vast swathes of America, Europe and Australasia. Even though rules around marriage in many of these places have relaxed, allowing people to marry more than once, women to marry women and men to marry men, tradition still rules when it comes to this particular part of the institution. But why?

In some places, changing your name when you marry is no longer the norm, due to progressive laws and attempts to move toward gender equality. In Quebec, Canada, women have had to keep their maiden names after marriage since 1981; in Greece, since 1983.

At the other end of the spectrum are countries such as the UK, USA and Australia, where more women still take their husband's name than those who don't, despite it not being a legal requirement. In Japan, it is actually law that married couples take one of the spouses' family names. Only 4 per cent of men take their wife's name. Surprise, surprise.

What's in a name?

Historically, in these places, changing your name signified you joining a new family (or being sold to them, essentially). A woman was a piece of property who assumed the name of her new "owner". But things have changed now, right?

Well, many modern feminists would argue that as long as marriage exists in its anachronistic form, it can never provide equality to a man and women in a heterosexual relationship – simply because it is, by nature, a gendered institution in which

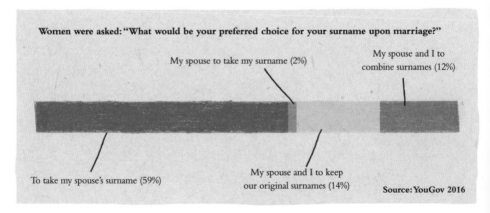

Women were asked: "What would be your preferred choice for your surname upon marriage?"

My spouse to take my surname (2%)

My spouse and I to combine surnames (12%)

To take my spouse's surname (59%)

My spouse and I to keep our original surnames (14%)

Source: YouGov 2016

wives give up their name, their independence and their freedom to become part of a patriarchal unit.

So yes, it is "just tradition" to change your name. But is it a tradition you want to be a part of? In 2013 research conducted by Facebook for British newspaper *The Sunday Times* showed that younger women are increasingly answering "no" to that question, and instead finding a middle ground by marrying their partners but not taking their name. The statistics showed that a third of all married women in their twenties chose to keep their own names, while only 12 per cent of women in their sixties decided not to take their husband's name; 62 per cent of married women in their twenties took their spouse's surname, while 74 per cent did in their thirties and 88 per cent did in their sixties.

But what has tradition ever done for me?

People still do a lot in the name of "tradition": leave their inheritance to their first male son; expect the bride's parents to foot the entire wedding bill; leave a woman to do all the housekeeping. You will notice a recurring theme here – in most of these instances "tradition" stipulates a situation that benefits the man, not the woman.

There are some alternative options: you could keep your name; you could persuade your husband-to-be to take your name; or you could even join your names together like many Spanish women do – or like Barbara Smith did. A leading mid-19th-century women's rights activist and member of The Ladies of Langham Place, one of the first women's rights groups, Smith didn't just take her French husband's name of Bodichon when she married, but added her own to his to become **Barbara Smith Bodichon** (1827–91). She was light years ahead of her time.

Another formidable feminist, **Kate Millett** (1934–2017), took issue with the coercive forces of the patriarchy, which demanded a woman sacrifice herself to her male partner. Throughout the 1960s and 1970s Millett gave the women's rights movement academic rigour, but also approached serious issues with a candour and honesty that helped bring the movement to the masses.

Millett made such an impact on the contemporary culture of the day that *Time* magazine featured her portrait on its cover on 31 August 1970. Book critic Christopher Lehmann-Haupt (b. 1934) wrote that her seminal 1970 work, *Sexual Politics*, was "written with such fierce intensity that all

"Patriarchy, reformed or unreformed, is patriarchy still: its worst abuses purged or foresworn, it might actually be more stable and secure than before."
Kate Millett

vestiges of male chauvinism ought by rights to melt and drip away like so much fat in the flame of a blowtorch".

Sexual Politics sought to expose sexist oppression, but also to demonstrate how culture, the stories we produce and consume, contribute to inequality. Millett wanted to achieve one thing with her book: to help eradicate the patriarchy. But she also recognized that the patriarchy must be brought down at the same time as the culture of sexism, which oppresses women.

And that is what taking your husband's name by default is: culture. Culture that says you should be part of a legally recognized couple, and that your personal, private life must adhere to the rules set out by generations of people before you.

Key consideration

Just because it's tradition, does that mean it's right for everyone?

Losing your independence

Changing your name when you marry is not really just a metaphorical metamorphosis. In many parts of the world, marriage would not be by choice, and it would mean the end of any sort of independence you had previously enjoyed. In these places it is still unusual for women to have their own bank account – the one thing, it has been suggested, that women need in order to achieve equality, independence and personal freedom.

The independence of women is something for which feminists have been fighting for centuries – to the point now that women are often accused of being "too independent". It is not possible for a man to be "too" independent, but now that women have careers and identities of their own, away from

their husbands, they can be "too". Worse, still, that a woman wants to remain independent – by keeping her own name, or by choosing to remain single and child-free.

When you marry, aside from changing your name, there are likely to be other personal freedoms that you will have to give up. But perhaps you want to give them up? There is no greater disservice done to the feminist movement than to make the assumption that a woman who wants to be a mother and a wife cannot also be a feminist.

American feminist writer **Betty Friedan** (1921–2006) was a complete romantic and, for all her criticisms of the traditional values that dictate how men and women live their lives, she still wanted men and women to be able to live together in harmony. She wholeheartedly believed in heterosexual love and marriage (although, it must be said, she was also, unforgivably, homophobic) and even joked that her tombstone should read: "She helped make women feel better about being women and therefore better able to freely and fully love men." Make of that what you will.

If you don't conform to tradition and take your husband's name, complications will arise. Society is not structured for a family with different names. How would people know you are a unit when travelling, for example? How will you prove your children are your children going through customs? These are valid concerns for many people, particularly when travelling to more conservative countries where couples may not be believed to be together if they do not have the same name.

Travelling abroad can, unfortunately, raise some issues if you don't have the same name as your children.

Making a decision:

Many marriages end in divorce, so maybe you will have that other name-change minefield to contend with one day, too. But maybe not. Marriage can also be steady and long-lasting. So the questions Millett would have you ask yourself are: is taking your husband's name going to challenge your identity as an independent woman? Are you taking it simply because of tradition, or because you want to? Few feminists would suggest that changing your name to your husband's is going to take us any closer to living in an equal society. But even fewer would want you *not* to take it, if that was what you truly wanted. After all, it is just a name. But also, it is *your* name.

My husband and I both work. So why do I have to do all the housework?

Judy Brady • Jill Johnston • Betty Friedan • Arlie Russell Hochschild

You are not suffering alone. Evidence overwhelmingly suggests that women pick up more household work than men, even if they have jobs. This is bad for relationships. Research shows that when men do more housework, their wives' marital satisfaction is higher and these couples experience less marital conflict. And yet wives are still often expected to take on the majority of domestic duties.

Can we really put this down to sex? Here, we can talk about sex in both meanings of the word. Firstly, because they possess vaginas, are women naturally better at doing housework than men? Women don't clean with their vaginas, so that doesn't seem to add up. But women do use their vaginas to create human life. While the husband is out earning money, women stay inside, keeping house. The Industrial Revolution, from the mid-18th to the mid-19th centuries, only accentuated this issue. Now, even though women can go to work themselves, the world has not changed in accordance, meaning that often women do more than one job: one professional, one personal.

And when it comes to sex – the sort of sex that creates the human life that women then look after in their marital homes – this has also been found to have something to do with housework.

Click-bait headlines often scream things like, "Men, Want More Sex? Do The Dishes!", as if clearing up after yourself and your family is a job that deserves some kind of reward. One report investigating whether men who do more housework get more sex found the opposite to be true; it appears that when it comes to making the beast with two backs, upholding outdated gender norms is more important than creating equal labour.

I want a wife

Some feminists have taken umbrage at how sex is often regarded as a woman's duty to her husband, so maybe that explains this research. If you are a good wife who does the cooking and cleaning, then you will probably make sure your husband is satisfied in the bedroom as well.

This sort of special treatment from a female partner even led one radical feminist to

"Most women work one shift at the office or factory and a 'second shift' at home."
Arlie Russell Hochschild

"My god, who wouldn't want a wife?"
Judy Brady

announce: "I Want a Wife". In the iconic satirical piece, published in the first edition of Gloria Steinem's *Ms.* magazine in 1971, activist **Judy Brady** (1937–2017) explains what she could achieve if she, too, had a woman whose sole role in life was to support her and make her life better. "I want a wife who will take care of my physical needs. I want a wife who will keep my house clean. A wife who will pick up after my children, a wife who will pick up after me. I want a wife who will keep my clothes clean, ironed, mended, replaced when need be, and who will see to it that my personal things are kept in their proper place so that I can find what I need the minute I need it." Brady perfectly captured the spirit of male privilege and finished her essay with a resounding: "My god, who *wouldn't* want a wife?"

What if no one had a wife?

Does everyone *really* want a wife? Maybe not. Some feminists of the second wave (*see* page 12) actually thought the "wife" should be done away with altogether, that the nuclear family was a patriarchal construction that held women back.

Jill Johnston (1929–2010), critic for the New York newspaper *The Village Voice* and author of *Lesbian Nation*, regarded the classic family as a feudal and patriarchal system that only benefits men. Johnston suggested that in order for you and women around the world to escape male oppression (and sole responsibility for cleaning the house) society would need to be rethought

entirely. Johnston spearheaded the extremely radical and controversial *separatist movement*, advocating that men and women needed to live apart in order to mould a new sort of society that did not require the oppression of one sex by the other.

Perhaps you like your husband a bit too much to suggest this solution. But you have got to give it to her, the woman had some very interesting ideas. She is the one you can thank for the statement that "all women are lesbians except those that don't know it yet". Compared to the sometimes glossy feminism of Gloria Steinem (b. 1934), Johnston's take on equality and women's rights was gritty, abrasive and not at all pleasing to the status quo.

The classic housewife

At the time, this status quo saw hundreds of thousands of women like yourself being charged with living up to the ideal of the perfect housewife. Conforming to the American dream sold to her by advertisers, this woman believes that if she has the right vacuum cleaner, she will be able to make her husband – and herself – happy.

If you have ever watched *Mad Men* on TV, you will recognize this woman as Betty Draper. And it was this woman on whom the grandmother of second-wave feminism, **Betty Friedan**, based her 1963 book *The Feminine Mystique*. For Friedan, the feminine mystique involved sexual passivity, an acceptance of male domination, and taking primary responsibility for domestic labour

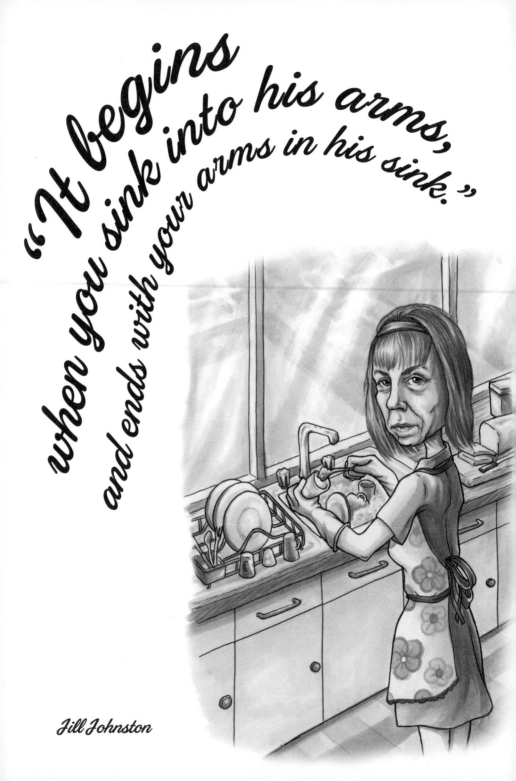

and child rearing. A woman of this mystique must provide maternal love for both her children and her husband.

Other heavyweight second-wave feminists, such as Germaine Greer (b. 1939), spent a lot of time on this topic, and they would most likely tell you that women are often so delighted to have caught a man (because society tells them they need one) that they will put up with almost anything.

The second shift

The concept of "the second shift" was first introduced by **Arlie Russell Hochschild** (b. 1940), who published a book by the same name in 1989. In it, Hochschild detailed her groundbreaking piece of sociological work in the 1980s, whereby she interviewed a number of women and their partners to understand the strain that was put on a woman who has to do two jobs. Many of these women were highly educated and had well-paid jobs, but still were expected by their husbands (and themselves, it must be added) to go home and fulfil another role.

Hochschild helped push this conversation in new directions by emphasizing that the uneven split of domestic work was not a "domestic" problem, but just something that had an immeasurable effect on the professional world, too. Women, she said, were required to make huge sacrifices, whether they were a housewife or a working mother.

Key consideration

What effect does your "second shift" have on your work life? This isn't just a domestic issue.

Making a decision:

The housewife pays a cost by remaining outside of mainstream social life, while the career woman pays a cost by entering a workforce that allows her little extra emotional energy to raise a family. You are damned if you do, and damned if you don't. The system as it stands does not work for women because it evolved through a time where women were simply playing supportive roles to their husbands who went out to work. While it remains like this, and you have to pick up extra work in the home, equality will never be achieved either in the home or the office.

Do I even want kids?

Germaine Greer • Adrienne Rich • Shulamith Firestone • Caitlin Moran

Any women who has ever uttered the words, "I'm not sure if I want children," will know that in most circles of modern life, this is still a taboo. Not want children? You can't possibly mean it. You'll change your mind when you meet the right man. You'll change your mind when your biological clock starts ticking. You'll change your mind when you have your own.

Yes, at a certain point, what you thought was a private decision between you and your partner will suddenly become the subject of public scrutiny in whatever forum you are in, be it with family and friends, at work or online (should you even try to share your own thoughts with others). Because even in the 21st century a woman who does not want children does not make sense.

But to counter this strange modern mystery is an interesting statistic. The number of women choosing not to have children is on the rise. A 2017 article published by *The Economist* noted that just 9 per cent of women born in 1946 in England and Wales had no children and by 1970 this number had risen to 17 per cent. It is not just a generational thing, either. Birth rates among women in their twenties declined by 15 per cent between 2007 and 2012, and one in five American women enter menopause without children in a 2010 study compared to one in ten in the 1970s.

These sorts of figures are often met with alarm. What will childless couples do with their time? Go on more holidays? Save money, go out more and get lots of uninterrupted sleep? Or are they planning on doing something more sinister, like secretly plotting to end the human race by denying it just one family's worth of offspring?

Germaine Greer (b. 1939) weighed in on this in her 1970 book *The Female Eunuch*. The ecologically minded Australian-born feminist remarked that, despite popular opinion, it is not a woman's duty to reproduce. And yet, that is what women – and men – are led to believe from an early age.

It goes something like this: you go to school, you get a job, you get married, you have kids. Women are caring and maternal and, once they have trapped a man, it is only a matter of time before they will want that man to sow his seed in them so they can begin to create a family of their own. Right?

Do men want kids more than women?

But is this domestic fantasy all an illusion? Don't just take Greer's word for it. A 2011 survey of single, childless people in the USA found that more men than women wanted kids. In the same survey more women than men reported looking for independence in their relationships, as well as personal space and room to pursue their own interests and hobbies. Men wanting kids and women wanting independence? Whatever next.

Another poll from 2013 echoed those findings, with more than 80 per cent of men saying they had always wanted to be a father or at least thought they would be someday. Just 70 per cent of women felt the same.

So why do we still believe that all women must want to have children and that motherhood is the only true calling of a female? Heaven forbid someone with a vagina had another agenda, such as setting up their own business, becoming a world-class athlete or running for president.

Adrienne Rich (1929–2012) brought this topic firmly into the foreground of feminist theory in her 1976 book. *Of Woman Born: Motherhood as Experience and Institution* is a far-reaching meditation on the meaning and experience of motherhood that draws from Rich's knowledge of multiple disciplines. Taking in anthropology, feminist theory, psychology and literature, Rich points out that motherhood has never really been understood properly in any of these fields. It is, indeed, a new field that needs to be properly explored.

However, what is not new is the use of women's bodies to control them. "There is nothing revolutionary whatsoever about the control of women's bodies by men," explains Rich. "The woman's body is the terrain on which patriarchy is erected."

She even goes so far as to consider what life would be like for a truly independent woman, who was not defined by her status as a mother or a wife: "But can you imagine how some of them were envying you your freedom to work, to think, to travel, to enter a room as yourself, not as some child's mother or some man's wife?…we have no familiar, ready-made name for a woman who defines herself, by choice, neither in relation to children nor to men, who is self-identified, who has chosen herself."

Rich is ultimately unenthusiastic about the potential of furthering the topic, though. "The body has been made so problematic for women that it has often seemed easier to shrug it off and travel as a disembodied spirit," she says.

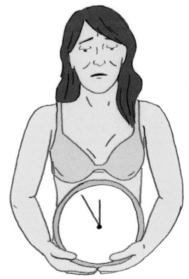

The "biological clock" has become a cliché used to lambast older single women.

Is being a parent a form of oppression?

Don't laugh. In an episode of Season 4 of the TV series *House of Cards* Robin Wright's character, Claire Underwood, was asked by a young mother, "Do you ever regret not having children?" To which she swiftly replied, "Do you ever regret having them?"

The topic of regretting bringing new life into the world is seldom discussed in public – presumably because there is no legal or moral way of getting rid of them. But for some feminists, children were just another way by which society oppressed women in particular. **Shulamith Firestone** (1945–2012) was one of six children, so presumably she had seen the burden that she and her siblings had put on their mother. The Canadian-American feminist was famous for reinterpreting Karl Marx, Friedrich Engels

> ### Key consideration
> Why do we still believe that motherhood is every woman's calling?

and Sigmund Freud in her first and only contribution to the canon, *The Dialectic of Sex: The Case for Feminist Revolution,* which she wrote when she was 24.

Simply, Firestone wanted motherhood abolished and for families to be reimagined in a way that divided the labour among adults of both sexes. She called pregnancy "barbaric", described childhood as "hell" and said giving birth was "like shitting a pumpkin". She never had any children.

Firestone thought the problem with childhood was the way it was separated so dramatically from adulthood, which in turn created a huge void in adults' lives – which they then tried to fill by having children. "An absence of contact with the reality of childhood makes every young adult ripe for the same sentimentalization of children that he himself probably despised as a child," she notes.

But perhaps Firestone's most famous and radical solutions were her ideas about artificial-womb technology. According to Firestone, the way families and reproduction work is holding women back. Instead

Do you ever regret having your children?

> *"We need more women who are allowed to prove their worth as people; rather than being assessed merely for their potential to create new people."*
> Caitlin Moran

of women having to have children, she suggested society needed technology that could allow children to be born outside of their mothers' bodies. This, she suggested, would be the only way men and women could ever truly be equal.

If humanity could reproduce itself without women having to gestate for nine months and then rear their children for 18 years, the world would be very different. Firestone saw this as a cornerstone of her feminist revolution. Perhaps it is an answer to your own question, too?

"You'll change your mind"

While you wait for science to catch up with Firestone's visionary ideas, if you decide not to reproduce, you will probably find yourself confronted by a lot of people telling you that you will soon "change your mind". English

journalist **Caitlin Moran** (b. 1975) has weighed in on this in her 2011 book *How to Be a Woman*. A chapter titled "Why You Should Have Children" was quickly followed by "Why You Shouldn't Have Children". In it, Moran said: "If a woman should say she doesn't want to have children at all, the world is apt to go decidedly peculiar: 'Ooooh, don't speak too soon,' it will say – as if knowing whether or not you're the kind of person who desires to make *a whole other human being in your guts, out of sex and food*, then base the rest of your life around its welfare, is a breezy, 'Hey – whevs' decision."

Making a decision:

The world does not need any more children, and it is interesting that many feminists have also aligned themselves with ecological causes. They would resolutely tell you: it is not your duty to contribute to our already overpopulated planet. Having children is a joy – but only for those who want them. But society also needs to accept new ways of women being women. Or, as Moran puts it: "We need more women who are allowed to prove their worth as people; rather than being assessed merely for their potential to create new people."

What is a normal family anyway?

Kate Millett • Germaine Greer • Shulamith Firestone • Sheila Rowbotham • bell hooks

In an age of high divorce rates, gay marriage and sperm donors, you will be hard-pressed to answer this question with any certainty. There really is no such thing as a normal family any more – if there ever was in the first place.

The stem family, or the nuclear family, with a husband, a wife and 2.0 children, was a concept built around the notion that the male parent provides while the female parent nurtures. It was classed as the ideal environment for bringing up children throughout the 20th century.

But it is a relatively modern concept. In many Western countries, until the 20th century, families lived in multigenerational houses. People did not have to travel great distances for work, and family units would operate together rather than being spread across the country or even the world.

Then came two world wars, and everything changed. People began to value their independence and women gradually gained more freedoms. The advertising during the second half of the 20th century glorified the family model of working father and stay-at-home mother, but gradually socialists and feminists began to question the foundations upon which this model was built.

By the 1980s queer theory was growing rapidly alongside the feminist theory of the time. With lesbian and gay liberation, which began in the late 1960s, male and female writers consistently attacked the common assumption that every household should be heterosexual and operate in a certain manner. And they were met with an attitude that in most places is still prevalent today: the nuclear family is a normal family. Anything else is "other". Whether it is lesbian couples, single parents or widows, society has always struggled to understand a family without a single adult male at the head of it.

The head of the family

Economically and socially this adult male, the father, was granted ownership of his wife and children, including – historically – the power to physically abuse them. In the US, for instance, "wife beating" was only made illegal in 1920 and it was not until the 1970s that domestic abuse began to be recognized as a serious crime, not just as a private family issue.

Throughout history, when it comes to matters of reproduction, it has been men who carry the bloodline. Therefore, the woman at the head of a family becomes a vessel and her female offspring of less

> *"The monogamous nuclear family has become such a preposterous ideal..."*
> Sheila Rowbotham

importance than her male ones. It is this thinking that informed the foundations for the contemporary family structure, and one feminist who spoke vehemently against this was **Kate Millett**. She practised what she preached by first marrying a man and then a woman. She did not do things by the book, and for this she was punished.

Millett regularly pointed out the social limitations of the male–female union, and saw the traditional family as a tool of oppression. "Patriarchy's chief institution is the family," wrote Millett in her 1970 book *Sexual Politics*. "It is both a mirror of and a connection with the larger society; a patriarchal unit within a patriarchal whole. Mediating between the individual and the social structure, the family effects control and conformity where political and other authorities are insufficient." For Millett, the normal family was simply an extension of male power, a private empire where the patriarchy could still exercise control over people's personal lives.

The socialist's solution

So if the family is a patriarchal tool of oppression, what to do about it? Some feminists suggested that instead of opening up the narrative to accept single-parent families, gay parents and so on, we needed a revolution. The 20th-century nuclear family represented a compromise; it needed to be done away with entirely.

Social feminists suggested that families should be more fluid and community-centric. **Germaine Greer** and **Shulamith**

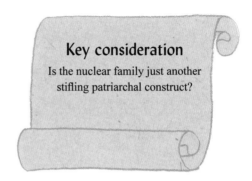

Key consideration

Is the nuclear family just another stifling patriarchal construct?

Firestone, for instance, both independently advocated alternative family set-ups where more than two adults shared the load of childcare, allowing more freedom and doing away with traditional gender roles. This is because the nuclear family, as Firestone wrote in *The Dialectics of Sex*, is an oppressive structure that perpetuates the battle between the sexes. Later, in *The Female Eunuch*, Greer imagined a time when men and women would be freed by less rigid structures, where extended parts of the family could live together and disrupt the traditional model.

This would help lighten the weight of family life, agreed British feminist **Sheila Rowbotham** (b. 1943). Rowbotham is of the belief that as the family becomes smaller in size, its emotional load becomes heavier. "The monogamous nuclear family has become such a preposterous ideal that it sags with the weight of its unrealized hopes almost before it creates itself," she reasoned in her 1973 book *Woman's Consciousness, Man's World*.

Co-operation between the family and the larger society is essential, otherwise neither would work. But if the set-up of our personal lives was adapted to suit more than just the man who is expected to go out to work and the woman who is expected to take on the majority of the childcare and housework, everyone would benefit. Family, these women argued, is detrimental to the community, weakening ties with relatives, friends and neighbours.

It's all about love

Another woman to join the conversation in her typically amorous, peaceful way was **bell hooks** (b. 1952). Family, hooks argued in *All About Love* (2000), was not the best way for people to operate. Rather, we should build our lives around love. She believed that it was community, not the nuclear family, that gave love and security to mankind. "Much of the talk about 'family values' in our society highlights the nuclear family, one that is made up of mother, father and preferably only one of two children," notes hooks. "In

bell hooks advocated an extended family model.

the United States this unit is presented as the primary and preferable organization for the parenting of children, one that will ensure everyone's optimal well-being. Of course, this is a fantasy image of family. Hardly anyone in our society lives in an environment like this."

Making a decision:

Like other feminists of her time, hooks suggested that the normal family was not just a tool of oppression, but also a gross oversight of how people actually lived, and particularly those who were not from privileged backgrounds. In her 2000 book *All About Love*, hooks makes the point that the isolated nuclear family required "material resources" that most people don't have: "The modern, idealized nuclear family is one available exclusively to the wealthy and the privileged." For open and inclusive feminism, it doesn't get much more real than that. The normal family does not exist. So go ahead and make your own rules.

"Patriarchy's chief institution is the family. It is both a mirror of and a connection with the larger society; a patriarchal unit within a patriarchal whole."

Kate Millett

Who should take parental leave?

Sheila Rowbotham • Simone de Beauvoir • Shulamith Firestone

The fact that you are even having this conversation means you are lucky enough to live in a country where the state recognizes that both men and women can look after their children. Congratulations! You are in a minority. In most countries around the world women take full responsibility for childcare, even if they also have to work to bring in an income.

Now for the complicated part. While some people may argue that bringing up children is a "woman's job", this has been hotly debated by feminists from time immemorial. Because, actually, many men are just as good with children as women are (and it is all subjective anyway).

Feminists care about this. A lot. It has been on the agenda for a long time now, in various different guises, because childcare encompasses a number of important areas in feminist theory. Maternity, biological essentialism, housework, capitalism, class, equal opportunity; each of these topics and more fall under the umbrella of parental leave. Motherhood, for all its magical qualities, is problematic for feminists on many levels, but none more so than the way in which it takes women out of the public domain and into the private one. It prevents a woman from working outside the home. It may limit her chances at work when she eventually returns. It holds women back.

So at what point did society decide that women were naturally better at mothering than men? Are "maternal instincts" just another construct of society's prescribed gender roles? When feminists critique motherhood, they argue that femininity is reduced to essentialist terms that assume that women are naturally selfless nurturers. These assumptions have meant society is structured around women being responsible for care – of children, of the elderly, of the sick.

These myths are constructed by the patriarchy, and they result in a world that restricts women from realizing their full humanity. In order for women to get even close to being on an even keel with men, childcare needs to be distributed equally. That is why paternity leave is so important.

Equal opportunity starts in the home

How can women take on more outside the home, without men adjusting their positions, too? This is at the heart of many modern discussions around what it means to be a man; if what it means to be a woman has been redefined in society, then men must also have their place redefined. Women disproportionately put their personal and career ambitions on hold in order to care for children and others.

According to a 2016 study of 22,000 companies around the world, countries with the highest percentages of women in leadership offered 11 times more days of paternity leave than those with the lowest.

All parents must learn to juggle, but mothers undoubtedly are expected to balance the most.

Researchers concluded that "women experience fewer disruptions in their careers and are more likely to make it to the "top" when men take paternity leave.

In 1973 socialist feminist theorist **Sheila Rowbotham** argued that unpaid work in the home and caring for children was central to the oppression of women. "Our labour in the family goes unrecognized except as an excuse to keep us out of the better jobs in industry and accuse us of absenteeism and unreliability," said Rowbotham in her book *Woman's Consciousness, Man's World.* "This separation between home and work, together with the responsibility of women for housework and child care, serves to perpetuate inequality."

More recently, a piece in *The New York Times* by two economists from the Brookings Institution put forward a similar argument. "The gender revolution has been a one-sided effort," said Richard Reeves and Isabel Sawhill in 2015. "We have not pushed hard enough to put men in traditionally female roles – that is where our priority should lie now."

Deciding whether you or your partner take on childcare is not merely a personal decision between the two of you, but rather, as these two positions highlight, a social, economic and political issue, too.

> *"Caring for small children is important and absorbing work, which does not mean that one person should have to do it all the time."*
> Sheila Rowbotham

But aren't women better at parenting than men?

Good question. Many feminists have argued that childcare is not an intrinsically female trait. Yes, you may be biologically designed to create the things, but as for caring for them all alone at home all day – well, what if your husband is better by himself than you are, or you are at a more important stage in your career? These factors and more need to be considered. It should not simply be a matter of, "Oh, I'm a woman, therefore I must be better at it."

Says who? Well, **Simone de Beauvoir** for a start. In her 1949 book *The Second Sex* the French feminist argued that women are repeatedly told from infancy that they are put on this earth for childbearing. They are told of the "splendours of maternity", and all the drawbacks of being a mother are overruled by the "marvellous privilege" of bringing children into the world. Such ideas, de Beauvoir pointed out, influenced women's ability to choose for themselves whether motherhood was even something they wanted in the first place.

Key consideration

To achieve equality, do men need to start taking on more traditionally female roles?

Rowbotham weighed in on this too, and through her socialist eyes she saw how capitalism had put housework and childcare in the same "female" category. "Housework is drudgery which is best reduced by mechanizing and socializing it, except for cookery, which can be shared," she wrote in her 1973 book *Woman's Consciousness, Man's World*. "Caring for small children is important and absorbing work, which does not mean that one person should have to do it all the time."

Why dads need feminism too

It is not just women who are held back by lack of choice. If women suffer from gender stereotypes, demanding that they stay in the home, so men face stereotypes that keep them chained to their desks. In the UK in 2017 it was reported that despite the introduction of Shared Parental Leave in 2015, there had been very little uptake.

Meanwhile, in the USA a nationwide Department of Labor study found that more than 70 per cent of new fathers took ten days or fewer off work, and of men who took leave only 13 per cent received pay, compared to 21 per cent of women.

Studies have also shown that dads who get involved in taking care of their children early on remain more involved going forward. And for those households seeking an equal partnership, both professionally and personally, being able to distribute the role of primary caregiver is critical.

Without paid paternity leave, fathers can't be equal partners at home, even if they want to be. And then there are the single fathers and the LGBTQ (lesbian, gay, bisexual, transgender and questioning) couples. Celebrating fatherhood with official paternity leave policies challenges traditional gender roles, promotes LGBTQ equality and empowers *all* parents in the workplace.

A radical solution

One woman with a really radical solution to this was **Shulamith Firestone**. Firestone wanted to, quite literally, take the weight of motherhood off women. She suggested that when science provided a way for the human race to procreate without a woman having to be in gestation for nine months, then, finally, women stood a chance at being equal to men. Firestone and other feminist theorists attempted to dismantle the social pressures put on women to "mother", and argued that this was a means by which society was controlling women.

To achieve sexual equality, men and broader social groups should take responsibility for childcare and commit substantial resources to it. Whether this is funded by a local authority, a support network of extended friends and family, or an employer choosing to allow women and men to work more flexibly or offer on-site childcare, it would benefit everyone, both socially and economically. This is particularly important for single parents and couples who are not earning much money – those who can't afford childcare but can't afford not to work, either.

Making a decision:

So when it comes to deciding who takes parental leave – you or your husband – what questions should you be asking? Well, the most obvious one is: who makes the most money? But there are a multitude of other factors. Who would be better at being on their own all day? Whose employer is more supportive of parents? Whose would allow for more flexible working hours? The more couples have these conversations, the more workplace culture will have to catch up with what people need, to retain the best employees. Here's hoping.

My daughter insists on being called "princess". Where did I go wrong?

Caroline Criado-Perez • Simone de Beauvoir • Kate Millett • Cordelia Fine

Is it a girl or a boy? It is the first question we ask when a new child is born. And that is just the beginning. Throughout childhood, children are encouraged to play with certain toys and act in certain ways that are entirely dictated by their sex. Is this right or wrong? And what happens if you just want to bring up your child to be a person whose interests and behaviours are not predetermined by what society expects of them?

Well, steady on there. This is centuries of social conditioning you are talking about. Boys do boys' things, like play with cars, and girls must surely want to practise their maternal instinct with little dolls, preparing them for motherhood and the caregiving role they will assume within society.

It is a tough one to pick apart – how we treat young people from their very first days on earth and how it influences their entire lives – but many feminists have valiantly tried. In her 2015 book *Do It Like a Woman... and Change the World* **Caroline Criado-Perez** (b. 1984) cites a study of birth announcements. In the study, the sociologist Barbara Katz Rothman (b.1948) found that the word "pride" was used regularly if it was about a boy, and "happiness" if it was about a girl.

Actually, if it was a girl, it was less likely that there would be an announcement at all. In some countries this is not just a matter of pride or happiness: girls are genuinely not wanted and are subsequently aborted, killed or given away at birth, simply because they are female.

Destined from birth

So are people really more pleased when they have a male child as opposed to a female one? That is a hard suggestion to stomach by most people's standards. Walk into any hospital in the developed world now and you are unlikely to find wives banished from their husband's side for failing to produce a male heir.

But whether we like it or not there are forces at work, both from society and within ourselves, when we are around young children. These forces mean that we treat boys and girls differently. And they dictate children's experiences and ultimately determine how they live their own lives. **Simone de Beauvoir** was ahead of her time in her musings on childhood and infancy, and eloquently discussed those malleable formative years of a young person's life. For de Beauvoir, the child's body was the instrument through which they first experienced the (patriarchal) world, and therefore any assumptions made about them due to their physical form would affect how they in turn viewed themselves. "Girls are pampered with kisses and treated more kindly, while boys will please by not seeming to seek to please," she explains in her 1949 book *The Second Sex*.

This, de Beauvoir said, was how young girls first came to see themselves, as fanciful objects that needed lots of attention. "If well before puberty and sometimes even starting from early childhood she already appears sexually specified, it is not because mysterious instincts immediately destine her to passivity, coquetry or motherhood," said de Beauvoir, "but because the intervention of others in the infant's life is almost originary, and her vocation is imperiously breathed into her from the first years of her life." Womanhood is nurture, not nature, said de Beauvoir.

What de Beauvoir touches on when she speaks of these "mysterious instincts" later became known as biological essentialism. This is the idea that your son's or daughter's essence is dictated by their biology. Also known as biological determinism, a popular example of this includes the notion that girls are naturally more maternal because of their genetic makeup. According to the *Encyclopedia of Feminist Theories* (2003), many feminists since her have taken issue with this, including renowned feminist biologists Lynda Birke (b. 1948), Ruth Bleier

> ## Key consideration
> Can we avoid treating children differently based on their gender? Or is it just programmed into us?

(1923–88), Anne Fausto-Sterling (b. 1944), Ruth Hubbard (1924–2016) and Sue Rosser (b. 1947).

One of the primary reasons they disagree with this understanding of human biology is that it ignores any outside forces that come to shape a person's perception of who they are, be that through the way they see their parents behave, what they view on the television, what they learn in books and so on. Children do not grow up surrounded by a blank canvas. The world is shaping them from the day they are born.

Is there any point in trying to fight it?

Assuming you don't fall into the "my daughter is a girl, therefore she must conform to society's expectations of her" category, you are on the right track. But

> *"Girls are pampered with kisses and treated more kindly, while boys will please by not seeming to seek to please."*
> Simone de Beauvoir

How do the toys we play with as children affect our adult lives and expectations?

still, it is difficult to avoid these pitfalls completely – as one experiment found out.

Conducted by the BBC, this experiment aimed to explore quite how difficult it is to achieve gender equality. The concept was simple: they swapped baby boys into girls' clothes and vice versa. Then, they invited volunteers to come into the room and play with the children, with a choice of different toys available to them.

Without fail, the "girls" were given soft toys and dolls, while the "boys" were handed cars and robots. The volunteers were shocked to find out they had walked into a trap and had, without hesitation, projected their stereotypes directly onto these infants.

This sort of sexism does not just occur in kindergarten. How many Disney films has your daughter seen that feature princesses? Girls, we are taught, are damsels in distress who must be rescued by a man. What can you do in the face of this widespread, institutionalized sexism that is showing your daughter only one path in life?

Kate Millett argued that female oppression begins in the home, so perhaps that is the place to start. If children grow up watching their mother be a parent and fulfil domestic duties, the chances are they are going to learn that that is a woman's job. Show them that being a pretty, domesticated pet is not a woman's job, or a girl's lot in life.

What toys teach children

In a more recent exploration of this topic Canadian-born British psychologist **Cordelia Fine** (b. 1975) tries to debunk the myth that men and women are hardwired with different interests. In her 2010 book *Delusions of Gender: How Our Minds, Society, and Neurosexism Create Difference*, Fine suggests that social and environmental factors influence the mind much more than biology (if biology does at all, that is – the jury is still out).

Some argue that because men and women are now equal in their rights in much of the world, there must be biological differences that are responsible for any remaining inequalities. That is rubbish, says Fine, and it really is time we stop using science to justify sexism.

So now for the meaty bit. Recent campaigns have tried to highlight just how sexist children's toys are. In most toy shops of the recent past, boys' toys and girls' toys have been separated, in case – heaven forbid –

a boy picked up a doll and thought it was for him to play with.

London toy store Hamleys famously become one of the first major toy stores to go gender neutral in 2011, but in many cases boys' and girls' toys are still kept separate, and toys are advertised exclusively to appeal to little boys or little girls. On the pink shelves you will find dolls and Barbies, encouraging girls to play with pretty soft toys that they can wheel around in mini pushchairs. On the blue you will find trucks, cars and robots, toys that in contrast have been shown to teach spatial awareness, confidence and an interest in technology.

Making a decision:

Research by the Institution of Engineering and Technology (IET) found that toys with a science, technology, engineering and mathematics (STEM) focus were three times more likely to be targeted at boys than girls. Pair this with recent figures showing that women account for just 9 per cent of engineers in the UK, despite enthusiasm among girls at primary school for information and communications technology (ICT) and computing. You can only draw one conclusion: the type of toys you give your children is affecting their chances in life. So if your daughter wants to be a princess, that is wonderful. Just make sure you show her that she can be a princess who also excels at mathematics and can pursue whatever path she wants.

Work & Pay

Chapter 4

I just want to be a homemaker. Is that OK?

Betty Friedan • Charlotte Brontë • Sandra Gilbert • Susan Gubar • Virginia Woolf

Feminists strive to give women a wider choice and more control over their own lives, and so would never suggest that choosing to be a homemaker is definitively "wrong". However, they might raise a collective eyebrow over this particular choice of unpaid career, as it has long represented a way in which women have been unknowingly coerced into doing more than their fair share of family tasks. Worse, into being a certain "kind" of woman – pure, noble and selfless. Angelic, even.

Domesticity has begun to have a glow around it again, at least in the Western world. Magazines that once used to produce articles for intelligent working women on far-reaching and complex topics seem to have swirled back to the 1950s. In place of articles on politics and careers, they seem to be drowning in celebrity trivia, "must-have" shopping items and experiences, and dieting regimes (often disguised as "healthy eating"). Crafts have seen a resurgence as leisure activities, too, with knitting and crochet becoming mainstream and practised by women (and a few men) of all ages. Recipes include time-consuming elements that were once seemingly joyfully handed over to the supermarkets – why buy your bread, these articles ask, when you could bake your own in just a few hours?

Hours? Given today's time-pressed culture, and the sense of constant rush and stress, how might anyone find hours to make bread? There is perhaps a clue in the winners of the 2016 Coupe du Monde de la Boulangerie – the bakery world cup. The three top-placed teams included 11 men and one woman. In covering the all-male Korean team's win, the BBC notes, "Men now do more cooking – at least when it's about showing off and public display." Feminist Delilah Campbell suggests in an article entitled "Housewives' Choice?" in *Trouble and Strife* that men have become the "public champions of private domesticity", ready to provide the celebrity and "expert" face of cooking.

The feminine mystique

Meanwhile, back in the home, things look very different. Studies show that while men are doing more housework, cooking and childcare than in the 1950s, when **Betty Friedan** (1921–2006) researched this for her book *The Feminine Mystique*, they have reversed since 2010, with women increasingly doing more and more on the home front. This is particularly true when couples have children and are juggling childcare with work. Full-time homemaking might appear to be a more attractive option – where this is affordable – but Friedan's 1963 book contains warnings that are still relevant today. When working full-time in

> "Had I not killed [the Angel in the house] she would have killed me. She would have plucked the heart out of my writing."
> Virginia Woolf

the home, women complained to Friedan of a general malaise, manifesting in sleepiness, inability to concentrate and depression. It stemmed from a boredom, she found, that was caused by the sheer lack of stimulation of working in the home, endlessly repeating daily routines (which is especially true for women with small children).

Given that the prevalence of major depression is currently higher in women than men globally (5.5 per cent of women to 3.2 per cent of men), and that research shows this does not change across social class, income, race, culture, diet, education or a host of other socio-economic factors, it might be wise to pause when considering homemaking as a career, given women's testimonies as to its depressive qualities. What's more, women have fallen into this trap before, in an era that saw similar upheavals in working practices, hours and wages to our own – the Industrial Revolution of the 19th century. The technological revolution we are currently living through is said to be giving rise to many of the same fears and uncertainties of the Industrial Revolution, where norms, traditions and even roles within society seemed disturbingly fluid, and expectations and duties had to be confirmed or redefined.

During the Industrial Revolution, three roles for women emerged: the new woman, the fallen woman and the angel in the house. The new woman was anyone connected to women's emancipation and suffrage; seen as a strange creature, she might still be tolerated.

The fallen woman, on the other hand, was ostracized by society. She might be a single woman having an affair with a man (married or unmarried), a woman with an illegitimate child, an unfaithful wife, an actress, model or prostitute. These roles have one thing in common: they are women who refuse to play by the rules that govern the third possible option – the "angel in the house".

The angel in the house

This curious phrase comes from the title of a poem by the Victorian British writer Coventry Patmore (1823–96), in which he praises the traits of a simple country woman called Honoria as he tells of her courtship and marriage. Patmore explores "The Wife's Tragedy" (Canto IX 1), saying that "Man must be pleased; but him to please is woman's pleasure". She does this despite his apparently intractable meanness, as Patmore suggests that

The "Angel in the House"

103

the wife "yokes her heart to an icicle" whose "each impatient word provokes another, not from her, but him".

It is the wife's job, Patmore suggests, to make her husband into a better man. She is "naturally" unselfish, gentle, unquestioning, graceful, sympathetic, self-sacrificing, pious and – above all – pure. These attractive qualities will act transformatively on her husband, making him (in today's terms) "the best man he can be". The poem was enormously popular, and the writer John Ruskin (1819–1900) took up the idea of the angel in the house with great enthusiasm. He firmly believed that a woman's place was in the home, caring for the family and household, while her husband's sphere was the public space, in which he could earn money and protect the family (this was another evocation of the "benevolent patriarch", *see* page 30). Ruskin explained in his essay "Queen's Gardens" : "Woman's power is for rule, not for battle – and her intellect is not for invention or creation, but for sweet ordering".

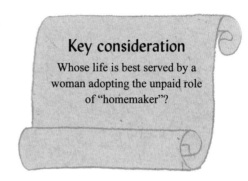

Key consideration

Whose life is best served by a woman adopting the unpaid role of "homemaker"?

The madwoman in the attic

One female author who would have disagreed with this idea was **Charlotte Brontë** (1816–55). In 1837 the poet Robert Southey (1774–1843) wrote her a letter in which he said that "literature is not the business of a woman's life, and it cannot be". Her lively riposte was the novel *Jane Eyre* (1847), in which she not only demonstrated considerable "invention and creation", but also imagined quite different roles for

women than those mentioned above. Jane Eyre herself is "quaint, quiet, grave and simple" but she also refuses to be an angel, even for Edward Rochester, with whom she falls in love. "I am not an angel," she says, "and I will not be one till I die: I will be myself. Mr. Rochester, you must neither expect nor exact anything celestial of me – for you will not get it, any more than I shall get it of you: which I do not at all anticipate." (There's equality in a nutshell.)

With her feet planted firmly on the ground, Jane Eyre becomes aware of a frightening figure that represents not so much her own opposite, as the opposite of the angel in the house: the madwoman in the attic. Feminist writers **Sandra Gilbert** (b. 1936) and **Susan Gubar** (b. 1944) found this figure to be intriguingly wild, with her purple-face, bloated features and dark, grizzled hair. Like the Jekyll to Jane Eyre's Hyde, the madwoman, Bertha, is only glimpsed at certain times of day, and represents a dangerously out-of-control version of womanhood. She was the Victorian nightmare: a woman who clearly defied all

> *"Man must be pleased; but him to please*
> *is woman's pleasure."*
> Coventry Patmore

the rules, norms and expectations of her time. The author Jean Rhys (1890–1979) reclaimed Bertha by writing her earlier history in *Wide Sargasso Sea* (1966). Here, Bertha is seen to be driven mad by being renamed (from Antoinette), relocated (from Jamaica to England) and placed in solitary confinement by a husband who no longer desires her. This was a common fate for women who actively refused to be angelic. Women who rebelled against the Victorian idea of womanhood found themselves labelled "deviant", "unnatural" and "mad", as

Elaine Showalter (b. 1941) demonstrated in her 1985 book *The Female Malady*.

For those who resisted more passively, a different fate awaited. In 1877 the medical text *Fat and Blood*, by American doctor Silas Weir Mitchell (1829–1914) suggested that women suffering from neurasthenia (a condition characterized by extreme thinness and anaemia) be given a rest-cure, consisting of enforced bed rest, isolation and force-feeding. This, he said, "could be used to discipline women whose illness became a means of avoiding household duties".

Making a decision:

For many feminists, becoming the perfect homemaker is perilously close to becoming the angel in the house. In a speech entitled "Professions for Women", the novelist **Virginia Woolf** (1882–1941) said that if ever you also feel that an inner voice is urging you to "Be sympathetic; be tender; flatter" and "Never let anybody guess that you have a mind of your own," you may, like Woolf, have to kill her. Metaphorically speaking, that is. After that, Woolf says, a woman "had only to be herself. Ah, but what is 'herself'?" That is the real question.

"We can no longer ignore that voice within women that says: 'I want something more than my husband and my children and my home.'"

Betty Friedan

Why am I working for less pay than him?

Jennifer Saul • Linda Babcock • Sara Laschever • Sheryl Sandberg
Sylvia Walby • Clara Lemlich

Women can be found working in virtually every job and career across most parts of the world. There are women presidents, surgeons, nuclear physicists, truck drivers and welders. At first glance, it might seem that women are enjoying equal work opportunities, with equal pay – so what is the fuss about? Unfortunately, despite laws aimed at preventing inequalities in the workplace, women earn just 54–79 per cent of what a man makes, in average jobs in the USA, for instance. Among the top earners, women earn just 39 cents for every dollar a man makes.

One of the problems, according to English feminist philosopher **Jennifer Saul** (b. 1968) is that women are consistently seen as childcare providers (Saul, 2003). This damages both young childless women and women with children, as the issue of childbearing and child rearing are seen to impact upon women's self-efficacy and potential. The selection procedure for any job favours those who can best fulfil the responsibilities of the job, Saul notes, and if women are thought to have (or might later have) other responsibilities that may interfere with those of the job, they will be downgraded in the process. As a result, Saul says, many more men than women will be offered jobs with good pay and benefits. The core of this problem is that it is difficult for women to liberate themselves from the cultural perspective and be seen as professionals, rather than women first, worker second. (This is another way in which women suffer from doing "the second shift", *see* page 83.)

Once in the job, women sometimes find it hard to ask for a raise, according to Microsoft board member Maria Klawe. She put this idea to Microsoft CEO Satya Nadella at a "Women in Computing" conference in 2014. What did he think women should do if they found it hard to approach their boss to talk about a raise. Nadella said that he didn't think it was a problem if women stayed quiet, because they could have "faith that the system will actually give you the right raises as you go along," adding that women would accrue "good karma" by not asking for a raise. His comments caused a public outcry, because feminists around the world believed that this example of benevolent sexism (*see* pages 30) actually served to hold women back.

Increasing self-worth

Negotiating is vital, according to **Linda Babcock** and **Sara Laschever**, authors of *Women Don't Ask: Negotiation and the*

> *"I am a working girl, one of those striking against intolerable conditions. I am tired of listening to speakers who talk in generalities."*
> Clara Lemlich

Gender Divide (2003). Looking at American statistics, they found that an individual who does not negotiate a first salary stands to lose more than $500,000 over their working life, and that men's starting salaries are about $4,000 higher per year than women's, just because the men negotiate. In addition, while in a job, women who consistently negotiated salary raises earned at least $1 million more during their career than women who did not.

Babcock and Laschever pinpoint two main causes. First, many women have been socialized to have low expectations of themselves and of success, and are therefore so grateful to be offered a job that it doesn't occur to them to negotiate their salaries. Second, in many cases women don't know the market value of their work. Research has shown that the amount women expect to be paid for a job vastly differs from a man's expectation of the same job; women covered by Babcock and Laschever's research reported salary expectations that were 3–32 per cent lower than men's for the same work.

Sheryl Sandberg (b. 1969), chief operating officer of Facebook and author of *Lean In* (2015) has acknowledged that she was coached by her husband and brother-in-law in how to negotiate a higher salary, as they were so surprised by her instinct to simply accept the salary first offered. She also notes that in her experience, women tend to hold back in meetings when they have valuable contributions to make, and consistently underestimate their self-worth.

Women don't apply for promotion until they have 100 per cent of the necessary skills, she says, while men start applying when they have only a fraction of the skills but far greater self-belief. Sandberg set up the Lean In Foundation in 2013, which also saw the founding of Lean In Circles, small groups of

Proportion of female employment in various industries

61%	Health Care
59%	Education
57%	Charity Sector
50%	Law
50%	Administration
50%	Communications
46%	Corporate Services
45%	Real Estate
41%	Financial Services
27%	Software & IT
25%	Energy & Mining
23%	Manufacturing

Source: World Economic Forum, 2017

women who would meet monthly to learn the skills that would bring them equality in the workplace, echoing the consciousness-raising groups of the 1960s.

Personal or political?

Many feminists objected to Sandberg's book, arguing that it addresses only the challenges faced by middle-class women, not the much larger number of women working in very low-paid, insecure jobs around the globe. It also seemed to view the problem as one that could be solved by individuals, rather than as a political problem that requires collective social action. Sociology professor Patricia Hill Collins (b. 1948) has pointed to the fact that the racial division of labour, institutional racism and different family structures put even greater pressures on women of colour.

According to the UN, the global gender wage gap was 23 per cent in 2018, and will take 100 years to close at the current rate.

Key consideration
Are men in the company paid more than you for doing the same job, or one of equal value?

The consistent way in which family demands and structures affect women's ability to achieve equal pay led sociology professor **Sylvia Walby** (b. 1953) to suggest that it is due to the intersection of two different types of patriarchy: one "public" and another "private". In her 1990 book *Theorizing Patriarchy*, Walby argues that women were at first trapped by private patriarchy, experienced in the patriarchal family. In this environment, women were necessarily dependent on a man (father or husband) in order to have access to the basics of food and shelter. In fighting for political citizenship (including the right to vote and access to education and the professions) first-wave feminists (*see* page 11) gave women access to "public patriarchy" – the capitalist world of paid work. However, the rise of capitalism and the success of first-wave feminism meant that capitalist employers greeted this new labour force – women – as a flexible source of cheap labour. And that view has been in place ever since.

As Shulamith Firestone (1945–2012) noted (*see* page 95), as long as women are the people who have the babies and carry the prime responsibility for childcare, they will be forced to seek flexible work that fits around those responsibilities and to take time off work to have children. This means they will inevitably be restricted in their job choices and will also be seen as "unreliable" by employers. Many feminists have investigated the phenomenon of private unpaid work (housework, cooking, childcare, care of the elderly, ill and disabled) with a view to solving this problem (*see* page 93). Philosophy professor Ann Ferguson (b. 1938) has argued that in an ideal society, this kind of work would be shared by men, either in the family or through state assistance, and pay for those in the caring professions – including teaching and nursing – would rise as a result. She points out that in stereotyping women as "naturally caring", it is easy both to assign them responsibility for unpaid activities in the home, and to underpay them for jobs that involve primarily "emotional labour".

"Women's work" is worth less

Many feminists have drawn attention to the fact that jobs which are viewed as primarily "female", such as the caring professions and support jobs (cleaner, dinner lady or canteen worker, and so on) offer lower rates of pay. However, if a job moves from being primarily done by women to being done by men, the pay scales increase dramatically – as happened in the world of computer programming (*see bibliography for studies*). And if women begin to enter any profession in

large numbers, as the Global Gender Gap Report 2017 states, "the pay-related benefits of participating in the profession declines". This means that although some countries have legislated to ensure "equal pay for work of equal value", the work itself seems to become devalued when women make up the majority of workers.

The idea that "women's work" is worth less has existed since women entered the capitalist workplace, and it has often fallen to socialist feminists to call attention to this inequality. In 1909 a Russian immigrant to the USA, **Clara Lemlich** (1886–1982), persuaded more than 20,000 women shirtmakers to strike for better pay, pointing also to the long hours, overcrowding and humiliating treatment that the women received from supervisors. Despite her success, one company – the Triangle Shirtwaist company – refused to implement the reforms advocated by the strikers and their union. Two years later the factory burnt down, killing 146 workers who were locked in the premises. "Triangle Shirtwaist" became a synonym for the working conditions of a "sweatshop" for several years, and women today continue to battle the conditions Lemlich fought in 1909. In 2012 factory fires in Karachi and Lahore, Pakistan, killed hundreds of workers – mainly women – in factories that were overcrowded and had no safety or firefighting equipment, exits that were locked or blocked, and windows that were barred.

> *"As she made the beds, shopped for groceries [...] chauffeured Cub Scouts and Brownies, lay beside her husband at night, she was afraid to ask even of herself the silent question − 'is this all?'"*
> Betty Friedan

Are you really working for less than him?

Philosopher Christina Hoff Sommers (b. 1950) has argued that the idea of the gender pay gap is fiction, because, as she writes in an article called "Wage Gap Myth Exposed − By Feminists", "the 23-cent gender pay gap is simply the difference between the average earnings of all men and women working full-time," and "does not account for differences in occupation, positions, education, job tenure, or hours worked per week". Far from confirming that there is no gender gap, feminists collectively point to Sommers's list and agree that therein lies the problem. It is not just a question of an elite group trying to break a "glass ceiling" or being unable to "lean in". Preventing women from accessing the full range of occupations and positions, denying them education, restricting their access to jobs or full-time employment because of their unpaid "second shift" and undervaluing "women's work" has led to women being trapped in roles that continue to see them consistently earning far less than men in every country in the world today.

Making a decision:

If you feel that you are being paid less than a man doing the same job or a job of equal value, check with your employer (or HR department), to see if there is a legitimate reason for the two of you having a different pay structure. If this is not the case, and you are being unfairly discriminated against, you can instigate an informal complaint or a formal grievance. If this fails to bring about a just result, consider mediation or making a claim to the employment tribunal.

Am I too nice to be the boss?

Rosabeth Moss Kanter • Alice Eagly

The concept of good leadership tends to be based on old-fashioned ideas about leading troops into battle and conquering things (countries, other corporations), so it is perhaps not surprising that *The Art of War* by Sun Tzu, a 5th-century BCE Chinese general, continues to crop up on aspiring leaders' reading lists. There are many problems with this approach, not least that it completely devalues "feminine" characteristics, leaving ambitious women in a curious double bind. Too nice: you are not a leader. Not nice: you are not a normal woman. Either way, "We don't want to hire you."

In 2013 Gallup conducted a Work and Education survey which showed that not much was changing on the leadership front: men and women who expressed a preference for the gender of their leaders (in work, politics or anywhere else) would rather have a man than a woman up front. This situation is unchanged since Gallup first asked the question back in 1953. Some things are changing, though, which is good news. First, people under 35 years of age were much less likely to be bothered about the gender of their boss than older people. Second, when men and women had actual experience of working under a female boss, their prejudices disappeared, along with any preference for a particular gender.

Token women

So, in general, things are moving in the right direction. However, as things stand today, your niceness may be problematic. That is because there are very few women in top positions in big organizations around the world – in politics, commercial ventures and even religions. In 1977 American professor

Rosabeth Moss Kanter (b. 1943) published a groundbreaking book called *Men and Women of the Corporation*, which examined the experiences of women in upper management of a Fortune 500 company. Although Kanter's book was published 40 years ago, her findings were found to be true of any firm or institution in which fewer than 15 per cent of the top positions are filled by women. Since this is still true of almost every organization, her findings are still considered highly relevant for understanding the current situation.

These rare women in high positions are viewed as "tokens" within the organization, and as a result they come under particular types of pressure (any increased "tokenistic" value, such as being different from the dominant race or creed, heightens the ensuing pressures still further). Token women, Kanter found, experience a heightened sense of visibility and attention that is not useful, as it leads to increased performance pressures and a felt need to stifle any emotional expression (which will be exaggerated in the perceptions of those around her).

> *"Leadership that brings peace is far more courageous than the one which opens fire and goes for war."*
>
> Asma Jahangir

Second, they feel socially isolated from other employees: the differences between themselves and the men (dominant in number) were exaggerated and led to rejection, while at the same time they felt disconnected from other women in the company. Third, token women realized that they were falling prey to gender stereotypes and expectations, which did not work in their favour. Kanter started to look at these in detail, and the four categories or roles that regularly cropped up in these situations may hold the answer to your question.

Pet, Mother, Seductress or Iron Maiden?

When there are a small number of women in management roles within an organization, Kanter found that co-workers and supervisors who are not used to working with women in authority try to typecast them into one of four stereotypes. Of these, three – the Pet, Mother and Seductress – are ones in which the woman is viewed as "acceptable" to men, but also as essentially incompetent. The fourth – the Iron Maiden – is a role in which a woman *is* seen as competent, but because she is "not nice" or in any way demonstrates "feminine" characteristics she is also seen as abnormal and strange (and therefore not entirely trustworthy). Margaret Thatcher (1925–2013), the only woman to have been Prime Minister of the UK when Kanter was writing, was publicly described as an Iron Lady (a variation of Maiden). The title passed to Germany's Angela Merkel (b. 1954) in 2005, when she was running for leadership of the country as chancellor. The strangeness of "Germany's Iron Maiden" was pointed out in detail by the UK's *Daily Telegraph* newspaper:

Pet　　　　　Mother　　　　　Seductress

When women reach higher-ranking jobs, the men around them tend to stereotype them into roles that make them more acceptable to them, and no longer a threat.

"She is viewed in her party as slightly eccentric – a remarried, childless woman of protestant stock who presides over a male-dominated, predominantly Catholic union." (This "eccentric" woman had topped the Forbes list of the 100 most powerful women in the world 12 times by 2017, when she topped it for the seventh consecutive year.) In 2009, when first running for President of the USA, Hillary Clinton (b. 1947) was described as an "Iron Maiden", and came under fire for wearing trouser suits and demonstrating "a lack of warmth".

These women focused on getting results and being effective, but they were perceived as not focusing enough on relational qualities to suit the male power structure. They didn't "fit in" the way a woman should. They seemed "too authoritative", "unyielding", and "made of iron – not flesh and blood". They have been viewed as unnaturally virilized ("having balls") and "could easily be a man" (this normally being a good thing in a leader, but not when the leader is a woman). These women attract large numbers of epithets traditionally applied to the warrior goddesses Medusa or Kali – they are "scary", "mean", "hard", "bossy bitches" or "bully broads".

If this is the only kind of woman viewed as competent in top levels of organizations,

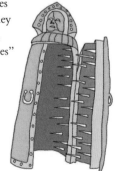

Inspiration for the term "iron maiden"

> ### Key consideration
> Is it possible for an aspiring woman leader to be seen as herself, rather than be forced into a stereotype?

it is understandable that women might shy away from stepping up. However, it is possible that you might not like the "nicer" stereotypes that these ambitious women find themselves forced into, either. The Pet is a woman who makes it onto the board of a company that rarely admits women this far. Her threat level is reduced by referring to her appointment as tokenistic, and acting as though she is a kind of mascot. She is treated as an amusement, generally liked but seen as incompetent, and she is not on the board as a serious player (according to the men around her). Diminished by being seen as naive or childlike, the Pet finds herself the butt of teasing and mock-abuse. She is patronized as "funny", "a laugh", "cute" and "a good sport" (but essentially "girly"). She might be a favourite of the boss, in a "cute pet" kind of way, who can easily be brushed aside when not "amusing" any more.

A token woman may be characterized in the Mother role by people who insist on noticing only her caring, nurturing side by seeking her out for comfort and sympathy. The threat that this woman might pose to

> *"Whether I am meant to or not, I challenge assumptions about women."*
> Hillary Clinton

those who are in competition with her is neutralized by positioning her in this way; she is not even sexually threatening. When she does try to exert authority, those around her act as though she is an overbearing schoolmistress, who is both boring and bossy, while also essentially frumpy. The Mother/Schoolmistress is too parental and humourless to be "the boss" and too nice to be a leader, so her stereotype, while having some capability, still prevents her from taking a key leadership role.

Lastly, if a woman in a high-ranking position uses her good relational skills to build alliances within the company, she may find herself dismissed as a Seductress. The implication here is that she is "sleeping with the boss" (or trying to); a "vamp" who "eats men for breakfast". This stereotype gives people a way of using a woman's attractiveness as a way of dismissing her abilities.

Making a decision:

The main problem here lies, as so often, with the cultural demand for women to be "nice". Women are expected by society to exhibit "communal" qualities. such as compassion and sensitivity. Leaders, on the other hand, are expected to exhibit behaviours such as dominance, agency and competitiveness ("agentic" behaviours), traditionally associated with masculinity. So if you conform to the culturally prevailing ideas of womanhood, you will be seen as too nice to be a leader. But if you exhibit agentic behaviours, you will be viewed as "ballsy" but socially deficient. However, as professor of management and organizations, **Alice Eagly** (b. 1938) has shown that the more women that fill top positions, the more people experience women as the boss, with a resulting disappearance of stereotypes and an increase of confidence in women leaders in general. So perhaps you can be nice and get to the top (you might have to wait for a few years, though).

When I was renegotiating my salary, my boss said he was "aware he might be dazzling me with percentages". What is he thinking?

Phyllis Chesler • Judith Sargent Murray • Olympe de Gouges •
Mary Wollstonecraft • Malala Yousafzai

You have touched upon one of the most enduring ideas men have used to "keep women in their place" – namely, that men are rational, while women are emotional and incapable of rational thought. This dates back at least as far as Aristotle (384–322 BCE), who wrote in *The History of Animals* that a woman's "natural life" should be focused on nurturing children and preserving possessions acquired by her "natural ruler", because she is "more impulsive...more jealous, more querulous, more apt to scold and to strike."

There is much in that statement for feminists to argue with, but the point that seems most relevant to your boss's comment is the assumed lack of rationality in a woman. Your boss implies this and then builds on this belief to presume a further point, which is that you won't be able to do mathematics. This idea never seems to lose traction, and it is not uncommon today – in any country – to read headlines such as this: "Why boys are better at exams". For those who take the trouble to read the full articles behind the headlines, the story often turns out to be quite surprising. The UK's *Daily Telegraph* published an article with this headline in 2013, in which an admissions officer for Oxford University explains that this is because "male students will generally go with their gut feeling. Girls will try and reason it out". It is tempting to repeat that last sentence. But the damage is done; the

screaming headlines go viral, and girls find themselves predictably patronized.

The idea that women lack rationality is a dangerous one because it sits on a continuum, one end of which is the idea that girls and women are "a little bit emotional" and the other end is the notion that women are always only a hair's breadth away from being "crazy". By 1859 doctors in Europe were claiming that a quarter of all women suffered from hysteria, which resulted in the large-scale imprisonment of women in asylums. This proved to be a useful "reason" for men wanting to remove wives or daughters, from their daily lives, as documented by **Phyllis Chesler** (b. 1940) in her 1972 book *Women and Madness*. The situation is much improved today, but Google still offers up plenty of websites on the subject of "why women are crazy", as if the truth of the idea is taken for granted.

> *"For my brothers it was easy to think about the future. They can be anything they want."*
>
> Malala Yousafzai

Where did this idea come from?

The current cycle of the idea that women are irrational seems to date back to the Enlightenment – a philosophical movement in the 18th century that was also known as the Age of Reason. For the first time, people in Europe began to vigorously question the authority of the Church (especially the Catholic Church) and turn instead to science for answers. One of its main proponents, Jean-Jacques Rousseau (1712–78), was to become famous for influencing the French Revolution, having roused the nation by beginning his 1762 book, *The Social Contract*, with the words, "Man is born free, and everywhere he is in chains." However, it soon became clear that when Rousseau said "man", he was not implying women as well – he seriously meant "men" only. In another book of the same year, *Émile*, he wrote specifically about the need to enchain women: "Always justify the burdens you impose on girls but impose them anyway... They must be thwarted from an early age."

Rousseau justified this by explaining what women are "naturally" like, without any sense of noticing that his summary had any kind of agenda. "Men and women are not equal," he said, "it is the part of one to be active and strong, the other to be passive and weak. Woman is intended to please man and their education must be wholly directed to give [men] pleasure, and to be useful to them." Unfortunately, there were not many women in a position to counter

this statement publicly at the time, but there were a few, including **Judith Sargent Murray** (1751–1820) in the USA, **Olympe de Gouges** (1748–93) in France and **Mary Wollstonecraft** (1759–97) in England. All three were self-taught, with de Gouges noting, "Fate left me in total darkness, in the most enlightened century." Wollstonecraft refused to accept that it was "fate" holding women back. If the Enlightenment's male intellectuals had noticed that women lacked education, and so found themselves unable to gain the same level of reasoning as men, surely the answer was to educate them? This idea was predictably and fiercely contested by male intellectuals.

Strangely perhaps, Rousseau was a close friend of Wollstonecraft's, and she countered his misogyny in similar terms to those Rousseau had used against women. "It is impossible to pursue his simple descriptions without loving the man," she said, "in spite of the weakness of character that he himself depicts." Women were going to have to aim much higher than men allowed and than

women themselves had deemed necessary up to this point. It was in men's interests to keep women as "empty-headed playthings", she said, because it afforded them control – of pretty much everything.

Malala – the cost of education

Once the education of girls and women had been identified as a key driver toward independence, things began to move relatively quickly in countries that had already recognized education as a common good. Progress has been slow, however, and today, girls and women are still widely discriminated against in terms of education. Two-thirds of the world's illiterate adults are women. Girls may be prevented from going to school through pregnancy, poverty, child marriage, gender norms, or school-based violence or sexual harassment – either at school or while travelling to or from it. In 2009, 11-year-old Pakistani schoolgirl **Malala Yousafzai** (b. 1997) spoke out on BBC Urdu about how important it was for girls like her to go to school, in spite of a Taliban edict the year before banning all female education. One day, as she travelled home on the school bus, Taliban insurgents boarded the bus

Key consideration

If we prize science and reason, who gains from the pretence that these are solely the preserves of men?

looking for her, and shot her through the head. She survived, after being flown to a military hospital in Peshawar where she was treated by an international team of specialists. One paediatric intensive-care specialist was initially worried about participating on security grounds, but then decided to ignore her fears. "She'd been shot because she wanted an education, and I was in Pakistan because I'm a woman with an education, so I couldn't say no," she said. Malala recovered, and in 2014 was awarded the Nobel Peace Prize. Five years after being shot, she took up a place at Oxford University, in a college called Lady Margaret Hall – the first in the university to offer places to women, in 1879.

Making a decision:

Knowledge is power. Perhaps this explains men's attempts throughout the world, over many centuries, to prevent education falling into women's hands. And if women do get an education? Just pretend they didn't. And that they probably can't do mathematics.

"Dismiss then those pretty feminine phrases, which the men condescendingly use to soften our slavish dependence"

Mary Wollstonecraft

My boss is insisting I wear high heels to work. Is this legal?

Nicola Thorp • Jennifer L Levi

In December 2015 temporary receptionist **Nicola Thorp** was shocked when her supervisor at a London financial centre told her that her flat shoes were unacceptable, and that she had to go out and buy shoes with a heel of 5–10cm (2–4in). When Thorp refused to do so, she was sent home without pay. Citing discrimination, she raised a petition that forced the UK government to rule on whether companies could enforce the wearing of high heels. The answer was yes, they can.

Thorp's case attracted a huge amount of attention in the UK, both online and in the government committee rooms, as hundreds of women came out with stories of being made to "dye their hair blonde", wear "revealing clothes" or "constantly reapply makeup". The formal inquiry concluded that the firm had broken the law, but in response the government said that despite the inquiry uncovering practices "which appear sexist, unacceptable and potentially unlawful... the scope for redress already exists" under the Equality Act 2010. As the Act states that in fact an employer has the right to distinguish between dress codes for men and women, they can specify clothing items for both genders (even heels). The one thing an employer must not do, within the dress code, is to be seen to be treating one sex more or "less favourably".

It is hard to see when that clause might be successfully cited in a court case, unless, for instance, a woman was made to wear a short skirt in freezing weather conditions, such as occurred in a 2016 case, when the UK's Unite trade union represented female members of British Airways' crew who wanted the freedom to wear trousers. This was forbidden under the BA dress code, unless a woman could claim exemption for religious or medical reasons. After winning the case, a union spokesperson pointed out that female cabin crew would "no longer have to shiver in the cold, wet and snow of wintery climates, but also can be afforded the protection of trousers at destinations where there is a risk of malaria or the Zika virus".

Taking the case to court

Professor of Law **Jennifer L Levi** pointed out in *The Yale Journal of Law &Feminism* that it is always hard to defeat sexually exploitative dress requirements in court for two reasons. First, a court may recognize the possibility of individual harm, but they require a group-based demonstration of harm in order to defeat a dress code on grounds of gender discrimination. Second, the courts are likely to dismiss a challenge out of hand by completely rejecting the claim that something socially "normal" or acceptable (such as high heels) could be pernicious. In everyday life, women freely choose to wear high heels, don't they? So what's the problem?

Levi also points out that although courts tend to see most sex-based practices as presumptively illegal, they view dress codes the other way around. It is up to the litigant (if she has the money to sue) to prove that the dress code is not just differential, but harmful, and more burdensome for women than are the dress requirements for men.

What's wrong with dress codes?

The corporate and government point of view, which is shared by some employees, is that a dress code is really there to guide employees toward an appropriate way of dressing for work. However, since these "guides" can be completely prescriptive, women may find themselves being forced to dress in a way that they find very uncomfortable. According to *The New York Times* (25 January 2017), one retail worker said that her firm encouraged female employees to wear shorter skirts and unbutton their blouses a little more during December, "when a higher proportion of male shoppers was anticipated". Which takes us toward an idea of the gaze in question:

whose eyes are to be pleased by alighting on women dressed in a society's ideal of the "feminine"? Whether this is a woman clothed head to foot in a burka or scantily clad in a bikini? And where did this whole idea of a "right way of dressing" come from?

Slut-shaming, Roman style

It turns out that the Ancient Romans have a lot to answer for. Until around the third century BCE women and men both wore togas, but in 215 BCE the law known as *Lex Oppia* was passed. This law prevented women from owning more than half an ounce of gold (which historians see as tantamount to requisitioning women's wealth) and stipulated what kind of clothes they should wear. A married woman was now to wear a full-length tunic known as a *stola* (New York Harbor's Statue of Liberty wears one of these). Under the Romans, prostitutes and slaves were supposed to wear *togas*, so that anyone could tell, at a glance, whether a woman was "respectable" or not. The *stola* signified married feminine virtue (the "good" woman), while a *toga* was possibly the first form of "slutty" female dress. The idea was introduced to mark out one man's property from another's (preventing awkward and accidental pick-up lines to another man's wife). In addition, it was a worse offence

"I could give a speech on nuclear power and newspapers would write about why I didn't wear earrings."
Pat Schroeder

for a man to sexually assault a woman in a *stola* than one in a *toga*. This ancient ruling introduced an myth that has been there ever since: the way a woman dresses tells you whether she is "available" and "up for it" or not.

Women were not happy about this new trend, and the historian Livy said that by 195 BCE women "beset the doors of the house of the tribunes" in an effort to get the law repealed. Ancient Greece was similarly concerned with regulating women's dress, and many states appointed "controllers of women" – a group of male magistrates whose job was to check women's clothing and enforce dress codes. They could confiscate clothing, impose fines or rip the clothing off a woman – in much the same way as police did in the South of France in 2017, when 20 towns introduced a burkini (full-body swimwear) and hijab (headscarf) ban. Photos began to emerge on Twitter of armed police surrounding a woman and forcing her to undress in front of hundreds of strangers on a beach in Nice. Onlookers used the hashtag #WTFFrance to

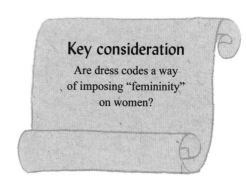

Key consideration

Are dress codes a way of imposing "femininity" on women?

question the validity, necessity and wisdom of these actions.

The name "burkini" comes from a combination of "burka" and "bikini", reflecting not only the item's waterproof capabilities, but also neatly encapsulating the two opposing ways in which men have sought, through law, to make women cover up more – or less. Hanane Karimi, leader of a feminist Muslim collective, points out that secularity in France operates with the same dogmatic force as religions elsewhere, "and it has the exact same logic in respect to the control of women's bodies". Between the eras of Ancient Rome and contemporary

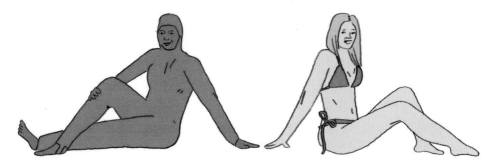

Dress codes often require women to dress in an extreme fashion, either entirely covered or barely covered at all.

> *"I refused to work for a company that expected women to wear makeup, heels and a skirt. This is unacceptable in 2017."*
>
> Nicola Thorp

France, there have been countless attempts to regulate women's dress, veering between the need to cover women more (because, the reasoning often goes, men are unable to contain their desires if too much skin is on show) or make them reveal more (and increase retail sales, for example). And the way the pendulum swings is connected to the men's use of these women. Men who wish to "protect" wives in their community from other men's gazes have introduced clothing rules and 24-hour curfews to limit these women's exposure. Men who wish to profit from the exhibition of women's bodies, whether by draping them, bikini-clad, across cars and calendars, or sending them out in bunny suits to persuade clients to spend more on champagne, cast their eyes skyward when questioned and innocently ask, "What's wrong with that?" Hugh Hefner, founder of the Playboy brand, actually called himself a feminist, as if he were oblivious to the fact that the entire brand was built around men's pleasure.

Making a decision:

Studies have shown that female candidates who interview wearing more "manly" clothing, such as a suit, are significantly perceived as better for the position. Sadly, it simultaneously lines you up to be swallowed by the Iron Maiden stereotype (*see* page 113). Witness the many times Hillary Clinton's trouser suit was mentioned during the US presidential election in 2016. Pat Schroeder (b. 1940), the first female from Colorado to be elected to Congress in 1972, said in an interview with *Bustle* in 2017, "I could give a speech on nuclear power and newspapers would write about why didn't I wear earrings." In November 2016, newspapers commented ferociously on British Prime Minister Theresa May's leather trousers (which cost £1,000), without a word about US President Donald Trump's far more expensive Brioni suits (around $6,000). It seems that your boss can tell you what to wear, but you may have grounds to object. As with so many other work-related questions that arise for women, in practice it's often a question of deciding whether to strive for fairness and decency, or keep your job.

Must I go out drinking with male colleagues to get ahead in my career?

Trish Hatch • Rob Willer • Ross Macmillan • Rosemary Gartner
Beth Quinn • Jennifer Berdahl • Maxine Waters

This sounds like a fairly innocuous question, but the truth is, you are damned if you do and damned if you don't. What is more, you may not get the chance to decide. In 2017 it was widely reported that US Vice President Mike Pence has a personal rule on the subject: he never eats alone with a woman other than his wife, and won't attend events featuring alcohol without her by his side. He claims this is a smart defence against sexual temptation. Other men have had female colleagues fired for being "too tempting". So hold back on that drink for a moment.

Utah state senator Todd Weiler said that it was "disingenuous" to pretend Mike Pence was the only man thinking like this. "What's more wonderful than a man who is trying to honour his wife?" he said, admitting that he has the same rule. "I'm probably just a little bit old-fashioned." Women should be grateful that we are being so incredibly nice to them, is the message. *The New York Times* conducted a poll in 2017 which showed that 40 per cent of men in the USA considered it inappropriate to have a drink or dinner with a female colleague. Interestingly, an even larger number of women felt the same, but for completely different reasons.

The male view

It seems that many men don't trust themselves if left alone in female company with alcohol on hand. *The Salt Lake Tribune* repeated the poll on Utah residents and received comments such as this from male respondents: "I love my wife and I would never cheat on her, but I could. I think everyone needs to admit that to themselves." What is more, this temptation alone is enough to get a woman fired. In 2013 in Fort Dodge, Iowa, dental nurse Melissa Nelson was fired from her job because her boss found her irresistibly attractive and a threat to his marriage, despite there being nothing but a professional relationship between them. Distraught at losing a job that she loved and had held for ten years before the dentist "developed feelings" for her, Nelson took the dentist to court for gender discrimination. Her testimony was never disputed, but the court dismissed the case, finding that her job had been terminated "to preserve the best interest of his marriage" (which was fine) and not because of her gender (which would have been unlawful). It is hard to see how gender failed to play a part here and, as Nelson's husband asked when the dentist apologized to *him*, "Why would those thoughts even cross his mind?

> *"It's a puritan idea of the separation of the sexes, which I find worrisome – even somewhat disturbing. It means that people don't relate to each other just as another individual."*
> Claudia Geist

Why is he thinking of her as an object?" We are back in the land of stereotypes in the workplace (*see* page 113), where the Seductress stereotype may be applied regardless of the professionalism of the woman herself. There is also a fudging between "I can't resist" and "it's your fault for being irresistible" that often ends with a woman losing her job, or with men refusing to meet on a one-to-one basis with female colleagues (as per Mike Pence). As Clara Jeffery, editor of *Mother Jones* magazine, says, "If Pence won't eat with a woman alone, how could a woman be Chief of Staff, or lawyer, campaign manager, or...?" **Trish Hatch**, director of the Women's Leadership Institute, points out that casual interactions are essential for advancement in the workplace. "Those places are where you develop the bonds and the connections," she says. "When you're in a conversation with someone else and they say, 'Hey, do you know someone who could help with this project or be a good hire for this?', you're going to remember the people you have interacted with." Networking is an essential tool for promotion, but if men insist on refusing to talk to the women who aren't their wives at company functions, there is little chance of them accessing this route to career enhancement.

Given that men far outnumber women in management positions, there is also a real problem for women if those managers refuse to have solo interactions with them at work,

from a catch-up lunch to finishing a work project late at night. These are the times that employees can demonstrate their abilities and show that they are ready for promotion, so if a woman is barred from "standing out" in this way, she is unlikely to be promoted. On the other hand, if a woman is in a supervisory role to a team that includes men, this blocking of one-to-one interactions prevents her from being able to carry out her job effectively (while talking man-to-man is clearly fine). In fact, if every interaction between a man and a woman is seen as a sexual one, many completely everyday work

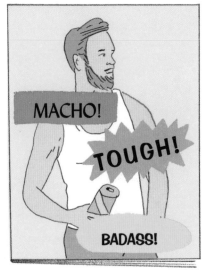

"Hegemonic masculinity" means that if a "man's man" is at the top of the sexual hierarchy, all women are at the bottom.

practices become impossible. So really (guess where this is going)...it's easier not to employ women at all.

The female view

When women are blamed, ignored or fired for being "irresistible", they generally see situations quite differently. If you were thinking of going out drinking with colleagues as a form of networking, you may now be wondering if your male colleagues are seeing things the same way. They may be viewing this interaction as potentially sexual, or they may not. And annoyingly, even if they don't, they may interpret your action as potentially threatening and react in a sexually demeaning way to "put you back in your place". Researchers, including **Rob Willer** (b. 1977), have put this down to "masculine overcompensation", which kicks into play when men feel their manhood is threatened, by social changes (such as women managers) or by someone questioning how masculine they "really" are. In response to this kind of threat, men have been found to start enacting an extreme form of masculinity – they don't just respond in a "male" way, but in an over-the-top masculine way.

For instance, in one experiment that looked at the way men and women shared digital

> ### Key consideration
> If you go for a drink with work colleagues, will someone else gain control of the narrative of "what sort of woman" you are?

images, researchers (Maass *et al*, 2003) found that men sent more pornographic and offensive images to women who identified as feminists than to women who labelled themselves as more traditional. Studies show that women who are considered "too assertive" in the workplace (or elsewhere) are seen as threatening the gender hierarchy, meaning that men feel their position "at the top" is in jeopardy. In this case, the most common form of denigration is via some form of sexual harassment (employed wives of unemployed husbands face a greater risk of domestic abuse, according to **Ross MacMillan** and **Rosemary Gartner**, 1968). Surprisingly, perhaps, this means that female managers and supervisors – who most

> *"Sexual harassment can serve as an equalizer against women in power, motivated more by control and domination than by sexual desire."*
> Heather McLaughlin, Christopher Uggen and Amy Blackstone

challenge the hierarchy – are more likely to experience sexual harassment than other working women. Even at the top, women are vulnerable, because sexual harassment reduces women to sexual objects, which sociology professor **Beth Quinn** says "may trump a woman's formal organizational power".

Sexual harassment

Professor of Leadership Studies **Jennifer Berdahl** suggests that we use the term "sex-based harassment" to discuss behaviour that derogates, demeans or humiliates an individual based on sex, because the behaviour is not "sexual" but controlling. She found that women who act in ways that are considered stereotypically male – being assertive, dominant and independent – are more likely to experience harassment than other women. So when men make comments about a woman's body or imagined sexual acts, or send a verbal or physical message of "check it out" to other men, they are acting to reinforce masculine dominance, by relegating women to the "low status of being a means to a man's sexual ends". This is why women regard sexual comments in the workplace, for example, as coercive, and not as men suggest they should: "It's flattering! Honestly! What's up with *her*?" In this way, men can both harass women and deny its potential harm.

Making a decision:

It seems that whichever way you go you will likely find yourself in an awkward position. If one of those men who can't trust themselves around women talks to you, be ready to walk away or lose your job. If you find yourself having a good time being "one of the boys", be prepared for some put-downs over the next few days to put you "back in your place". Don't be too attractive ("irresistible"), clever ("power-grabbing"), caring ("mumsy") or cynical ("cold bitch"). Perhaps take your line from US congresswoman **Maxine Waters** (b. 1938), whose arguments in the House were disregarded by Bill O'Reilly of Fox News because he was unable "to hear a word she said" because he was so distracted by her hair, he said. Waters' advice? "I'd like to say to women out there everywhere: don't allow these right-wing talking heads, these dishonourable people, to intimidate you or scare you. Be who you are. Do what you do. And let us get on with discussing the real issues of this country."

Do women have to be naked to get into the Met. Museum?

Guerrilla Girls • Mary Richardson • Linda Nochlin • Bettany Hughes

In 1985 a group of professional women artists staged a protest against the Museum of Modern Art in New York. At the time it was staging a show that purported to be the "definitive" survey of contemporary art, but of the 169 artists featured, only 13 were women. The protest was met with the same indifference as the work of women artists in general, so in 1989 the activists decided to use both female nudity and anonymity to make a point.

Taking one of the art world's most famous nudes, *La Grande Odalisque* (1814) by Jean-Auguste-Dominique Ingres, as the centrepiece for a poster, the **Guerrilla Girls** replaced the woman's head with a gorilla's, and added the question, "Do women have to be naked to get into the Met. Museum?" The protestors (who now appeared in public only when wearing gorilla masks themselves) had turned their attention to the permanent displays of the museum, and found that in the "modern" galleries, fewer than 5 per cent of the artists represented were women, while 85 per cent of the nudes in those same galleries were female.

They had found yet more proof that it is easier for a woman to turn up in history as a sexualized object than as a subject operating in the world with agency herself (*see* page 115). The Guerrilla Girls kept a watch on those galleries, and 23 years later found that the situation was no better: in 2012 only 4 per cent of the artists in the Modern Art section were women, while 76 per cent of the nudes were female. "Fewer women artists, more naked males," was their comment. "Is this progress? Guess we can't put our masks away yet."

Slashing art

If the Guerrilla Girls were restrained in their demolition of a famous nude, however, the same was not true of **Mary Richardson** (1882–1961), a suffragette who repeatedly slashed at *The Rokeby Venus* (1647) by Diego Velázquez in the National Gallery in 1914. This painting was said by *The Times* to be "neither idealistic nor passionate, but absolutely natural, and absolutely pure". Richardson, a suffragette who had been imprisoned ten times already that year and had endured force-feeding while on hunger strike, did not agree. To her, it was a representation of a woman, by a man, that modelled men's ideas of how women should look and behave. The ultimate insult was that this painting of a woman was seen as more valuable than a real woman. Richardson slashed the painting several times, saying afterward, "You can get another picture, but you cannot get a life." The difficulty, according to both Richardson and the Guerrilla Girls, lies in persuading the world to take women seriously and afford them the same respect as men. One question continues to crop up so often that art historian **Linda Nochlin** (1931–2017) made it the title of her 1988 essay: "Why have there been no great women artists?" Nochlin argued that women have faced so many institutional barriers when it comes to art that it is miraculous that so many works were ever made, let alone found their way into museums. Women have not had the same level of access to education, support (official or individual), public spaces, market places or social networks as men. Until very recently, all the significant figures in the art world – the curators, museum directors, critics, funding officers and academics – were male. The people who valued the work and marked it as "collectible" were male, and the commercial art industry thrived by servicing the appetites of the wealthy, who – given the unequal distribution of wealth in society – are largely male. This is a complete system that excludes women. Nochlin suggests that we have to see artistic careers not as the manifestation of "inbuilt greatness" but as the product of institutional structures.

Given the inequality of education, training and route to market afforded to women, Nochlin also suggested that we "stop counting" women's achievements, in an attempt to prove that women were capable of great things. And yet – there *are* many great women artists, and there always have been, despite that astounding lack of opportunity.

Recognizing women's contributions

In the 21st century historians across various fields are attempting to reinstate women's achievements into the history books. As historian **Bettany Hughes** (b. 1967) notes, women have always been around 50 per cent of the population, but they only occupy about 0.5 per cent of recorded history. She explains that from 40,000 BCE to around 5,000 BCE, women were very present in the archaeological record. They had property rights, could own land, could serve as high priestesses and could generally operate at high levels within the sophisticated settlements of the time. However, there was a "quantum shift" at around 5,000 BCE, when there was an alteration in the measure of success. Whereas previously a civilization was judged successful

Chien-Shiung Wu
(1912-1997)
Nuclear Physicist

Esther Lederberg
(1922-2006)
Microbiologist

Jocelyn Bell Burnell
(b. 1943)
Astrophysicist

because of its continuity, the new measure of success was expansion. This took military might and muscle. The shift is noticeable in epic poetry, such as the *Iliad*, the *Odyssey* and the *Epic of Gilgamesh*, which expound upon the new male hero and his conquering ways.

The role of women in history since then has been diminished in inverse proportion to the rise of the male role. And although women have always achieved in virtually every field, despite being blocked from educational and professional institutions, their contributions have necessarily been fewer. What is perhaps stranger is some men's need to then add to the problem by refusing to publicly acknowledge women's achievements, or even take them as their own. Even Egyptian queen Cleopatra (*c.*69–30 BCE) – a renowned mathematician, poet and philosopher in African and Islamic tradition – is "remembered" in the West for seducing two famous Roman generals, Caesar and Mark Antony. Neither Mary Richardson nor the Guerrilla Girls would be surprised to learn that after Cleopatra killed herself in order to avoid being paraded through the streets as a trophy by her victor, the emperor Augustus. He paraded an image of her through the streets instead.

Why do men always get the credit?

When Hungarian swimmer Katinka Hosszú won gold in the Rio Olympics in 2016, the commentator congratulated her coach as "the guy responsible for turning [her] into a whole different swimmer", rather than recognize the efforts of Hosszú herself. This "sliding of credit" from female to male has occurred countless times in history. In the 11th century, for instance, physician Trotula of Salerno was unable to retain the credit for her very well-known works. Her books about diseases and conditions affecting women were widely used as important medical resources but, over time, people began to question her authorship – surely these works couldn't have been written by a woman? Some texts were reissued with the names of male authors, while some commentators argued that many (male) authors must have been involved. Today, historians agree that Trotula did exist, was a woman, and did indeed write those works. It only took around 1,000 years for her to regain the credit.

> ### Key consideration
> How do we know what women have achieved, if their arts and inventions have been miscredited or lost?

> *"Women are always told, 'You're not going to make it, it's too difficult, you can't do that, don't enter this competition, you'll never win it."*
> Zaha Hadid

Nettie Stevens
(1861-1912)
Geneticist

Lise Meitner
(1878-1968)
Physicist

Rosalind Franklin
(1920-1958)
Chemist

The part women have played in science has been notoriously overlooked. The contributions of Chinese nuclear physicist Chien-Shiung Wu (1912–97) and Austrian physicist Lise Meitner (1878–1968) to the development of the nuclear bomb are only now being acknowledged, while the discovery by American biologist Nettie Stevens (1861–1912) that sex is determined by chromosomes in the male's sperm is still often credited to her colleague, E B Wilson (1856–1939). Wilson arrived at his conclusion after he had seen the results of Stevens's work, but as science historian Stephen Brush (b. 1935) notes, "because of Wilson's more substantial contributions in other areas, he tends to be given most of the credit for this discovery".

This is known as the "Matilda Effect". The term was coined in 1993 by science historian Margaret Rossiter (b. 1944), to refer to the way that so many accomplishments by female scientists have been historically under-recognized, while credit has been disproportionately given to male scientists. Its name follows a theme begun by the "Matthew Effect", defined by Robert K Merton in 1968, which states that already-prominent people are more likely to get credit than unknown people. Matilda effectively follows on from Matthew (in a way that is surely annoying to many feminists!).

Making a decision:

The historical record of achievements, largely written by men, suggests that women have not achieved much of significance in any field. If some are drawn back into the limelight many years after their deaths, the achievement is often presumed to have been misattributed. On the other side of this argument sit thousands of women who, despite being barred from education, denied financial and emotional support, and often completely banned from working at all, still managed to write, paint, discover, make and invent. Their work is being rediscovered all the time and rightfully placed in museums. And none of them is naked.

Women in the Media

Chapter 5

Dare I share my opinions online?

Sheila Rowbotham • Laurie Penny • Beryl Fletcher • Audre Lorde

The internet was meant to be good: a brave new world where people could interact freely and without judgment; a place where who you were, what you looked like and where you were from did not matter. That, as any woman who has ever dared to share her opinion online will tell you, is not what the internet has become. Not yet, anyway.

Social media platforms have been great for many reasons: feminist activism and Black Lives Matter, for example. For movements against transphobia, homophobia, racism and sexism, they have proved instrumental in changing the world for the better.

However, they have also provided a new place for groups of people to come together and abuse others; to spread messages of hate, or to send death threats to people they don't agree with. Most of the victims of this abuse have one thing in common: they are women.

A 2016 study by security firm Norton found that nearly half of 1,000 respondents had experienced some form of abuse or harassment online. Among women under thirty, the proportion went up to 76 per cent.

What are we talking about when we speak of "harassment" here? The kind you are likely to experience as a woman if you share your thoughts online could range from unwanted contact, internet trolling and cyberbullying, to sexual harassment and threats of rape and death. If you are particularly unfortunate, like one in ten of the women under thirty in this study, you could also experience revenge porn or "sextortion". And the discrimination does not stop there. The study also found the lesbian, bisexual and transgender women who had suffered harassment online were

targeted because of their sexual orientation.

What does this say about the internet? Or, more importantly, as author, blogger and cybercriminal expert Tara Moss (b. 1973) has asked in a 2017 talk (*see* quote above right), what does it say about human beings?

Why women – and why now?

Before the internet, people could express themselves in only limited ways. The media was largely controlled by big corporations run by men, and women were mostly portrayed by men. **Sheila Rowbotham** (b. 1943), the British socialist feminist theorist and writer, discusses this in her 1973 book *Women's Consciousness, Man's World*.

> *"This is not coming out of an abyss, it's not coming out of 'the internet', it is coming out of us. As a culture we are pouring our prejudices into the technology we use."*
> Tara Moss

"We [women] perceive ourselves through anecdote, through immediate experience. The world simply was and we were in it," says Rowbotham of the pre-feminist era. "We could only touch and act upon its outer shapes while seeing through the lens men made for us. We had no means of relating our inner selves to an outer movement of things."

But then came the digital revolution and, alongside it, feminism's fourth wave (*see* page 14). Anyone with open internet access, whose voices were not normally heard in mainstream media, could suddenly share their opinions and make themselves heard. English journalist and author **Laurie Penny** (b. 1986) has written extensively about these changes. In her 2013 book *Cybersexism: Sex, Gender and Power on the Internet*, she talks about the ups and downs of these new platforms. "The Internet made misogyny routine and sexual bullying easy, but first, it did something else. It gave women, girls and queer people space to speak to each other without limits, across borders, sharing stories and changing our reality."

Why we need women online

When the internet was first being used, many saw it as a utopia. Women, in particular, became interested in how the internet could help them fight the patriarchy. The term "cyberfeminist" was first coined in the 1990s, as technologically minded women began to gather in online forums, setting aside space in a male-dominated world of computer technology and asking themselves: can gender be escaped online?

For New Zealand novelist **Beryl Fletcher** (1938–2018), cyberspace had huge potential. In her 1999 essay for *CyberFeminism: Connectivity, Critique and Creativity*, she wrote that it can "stretch imagination and language to the limit; it is a vast library of information, a gossip session, and a politically charged emotional landscape. In short, a perfect place for feminists." If you fast-forward to now, it is clear that cyberspace is not a perfect place for anyone. As a result, people are increasingly censoring themselves online. According to the Data & Society Research Institute and the Center for Innovative Public Health Research, young women in America are most likely to self-censor, specifically to avoid online harassment, with 41 per cent of women aged 15 to 29 doing so to avoid abuse.

In each of these instances women are choosing not to use their voices, rather than face being abused. The onus is on the victim, not the perpetrator, to leave the

Key consideration

If you're silent online, isn't that the same as being silenced for being a woman in the analogue world?

> *"...but when we are silent / we are still afraid /*
> *so it is better to speak..."*
> Audre Lorde

space. As Laurie Penny puts it in *Cybersexism*: "We're saying precisely what we've said to young women for centuries: we'd love to have you here in the adult world of power and adventure, but you might get raped or harassed, so you'd better just sit back down and shut up and fix your face up pretty."

The offline consequences of online behaviour

The way people are treated online has direct and very troubling effects on their personal lives – online abuse is physically damaging. Of the women who suffer at the hands of online abusers, 55 per cent say that they experienced anxiety, stress or panic attacks as a result. They also reported facing psychological consequences, such as a lack of self-esteem and a sense of powerlessness.

This is nothing less than a human rights issue. Amnesty International conducted their own survey of women in politics during the 2017 UK General Election, because of the extraordinary amount of abuse women face on social media. The organization analysed tweets mentioning 177 women MPs active on Twitter in the run-up to the election and found that this issue predominantly affects Black, Asian and Minority Ethnic (BAME) women. The 20 BAME MPs running for office received almost half (41 per cent) of the abusive tweets, despite being outnumbered hugely: there were almost eight times as many white MPs in the study. This abuse was of real, urgent concern, they said, as it prevented women from taking part in politics or even voicing their opinions in public.

So should this fear of the repercussions put women off entering public debate at all? **Audre Lorde** (1934–92), self-described as a "black, lesbian, mother, warrior, poet", was around before social media, and even then, during the second wave (*see* page 13), women were facing similar struggles (*see* part of her poem "A Litany for Survival," above).

Making a decision:

To see this as the internet's problem is to miss the point entirely. As long as women in any public sphere are attacked simply because they are women, we will not have equality. The only thing to do is to refuse to be pushed out of these arenas. So speak up. Say what you think. Post that controversial opinion. Because, as Audre Lorde once said in her essay "Transformation of Silence", "Your silence will not protect you."

Why am I so obsessed with what female celebrities look like?

Naomi Wolf • Susan Sontag • Camille Paglia

From tabloid newspapers to glossy magazines to social media, images are increasingly driving public discourse – and fuelling the world's superficiality problem. Smartphones have become a part of everyday life – and we simply cannot stop watching. It might be their clothes. It might be their weight. It might be the colour of their hair, or the colour of their skin. People in the public eye face continuous scrutiny, not for what they say or do, but for what they look like. This scrutiny is undeniably directed at women more than men.

And so it has always been. In the wake of the British government passing bills to give every householder and women over 30 the vote in 1918 and over 21 in 1928, *The Spectator* argued that the women made politics "unreal, tawdry, dressy". This editorial approach – the one that says a woman's appearance is more interesting than her words and actions – still plagues not just women in politics but any woman who finds herself in the public eye.

From the style of their hair to the length of their skirt, what women wear seems to be the most important thing in the world. If you believe the newspapers and magazines, that is, who turn over enormous profits by sharing pictures of everyone from celebrities to politicians. The more extreme the story, the more "clicks" a headline gets online: a woman must look either "stunning" or "horrific" to make the gossip pages.

Women have always had a difficult relationship with the media. During the feminist marches of the 1970s, as American third-wave feminist **Naomi Wolf** (b. 1962) points out in her 1990 work *The Beauty Myth*, "Headlines read, WOMEN ARE REVOLTING. Women took in the way the movement was being depicted, and the caricatures did their work."

The first thing the media did was criticize the women for their looks. You would hope this would not stop you from considering what the women who were standing up for equal rights were marching for, that it would not distract you from their message. And yet, that is what happens. You find yourself becoming preoccupied with a woman's clothes, or how she does her makeup, and then comparing all women in the same distracting, degrading, destructive process.

As Wolf observes in *The Beauty Myth*: "Though many women realized that their attention was being focused in this way, fewer fully understood how thoroughly politically such focusing works: in drawing attention to the physical characteristics of women leaders, *they can be dismissed as either too pretty or too ugly*. The net effect is to prevent women's identification with the issues. If the public woman is stigmatized as too 'pretty,' she's a threat, a rival – or simply not serious; if derided as too 'ugly,' one risks tarring oneself with the same brush by identifying oneself with her agenda."

Seeing ourselves through a camera

The rise of platforms such as Instagram only fuel a narcissistic obsession with appearance. But back in 1977, one feminist forecasted the problems that mass media and access to cheap cameras would have on the world. "Needing to have reality confirmed and experience enhanced by photographs is an aesthetic consumerism to which everyone is now addicted," said **Susan Sontag** (1933–2004) in her book *On Photography*. "Like guns and cars, cameras are fantasy-machines whose use is addictive."

Sontag predicted how we would come to obsess over our idealized lives, and begin to see ourselves more fully through the lens of a camera than we can see ourselves in reality. But perhaps most alarmingly, Sontag does not see this as a passive act, but an act of aggression. "Images which idealize (like most

fashion and animal photography) are no less aggressive than work which makes a virtue of plainness (like class pictures, still lifes of the bleaker sort, and mug shots). There is an aggression implicit in every use of the camera," says Sontag.

She also suggests that the time we spend looking at photographs of others is, in fact, not harmless fun, a "guilty pleasure", but rather that, "In teaching us a new visual code, photographs alter and enlarge our notions of what is worth looking at and what we have a right to observe. They are a grammar and, even more importantly, an ethics of seeing."

Spend too much time seeing the world through other people's images, and you might start to believe what you are seeing. But these images are not reality, they have been edited. They are the world as someone else wants you to see it.

Why do I take selfies?

The rise of social media gave everyone – celebrities, brands and everyday men, women and children – the opportunity to speak to the world directly, without censorship or editing. And yet we choose to edit our pictures, with filters and apps, so they look more like the images we see in magazines

> *"Needing to have reality confirmed and experience enhanced by photographs is an aesthetic consumerism to which everyone is now addicted."*
> Susan Sontag

and newspapers and on television. We have become accustomed to pictures that present an alternate reality, and reality does not live up to it. Wolf says that this highlights a contradiction at the very heart of Western democratic principles. In *The Beauty Myth* she asks, “How do the values of the West, which hates censorship and believes in a free exchange of ideas, fit in here?”

Key consideration

Does focusing on what a woman looks like distract us from more important issues?

Many feminists have spoken of the male gaze, and the idea that women do not truly exist in a patriarchal society without men looking at them. English art critic John Berger (1926–2017) famously wrote in his 1972 book *Ways of Seeing*, “Men *act* and women *appear*. Men look at women. Women watch themselves being looked at.” This idea has only been exacerbated by the digital age. Far from allowing women to “own” their public image, and letting them be seen how they want to be seen, it has increased our voracious appetite for pictures, both the Photoshopped ideals of beauty magazines and the scandals of the gossip pages.

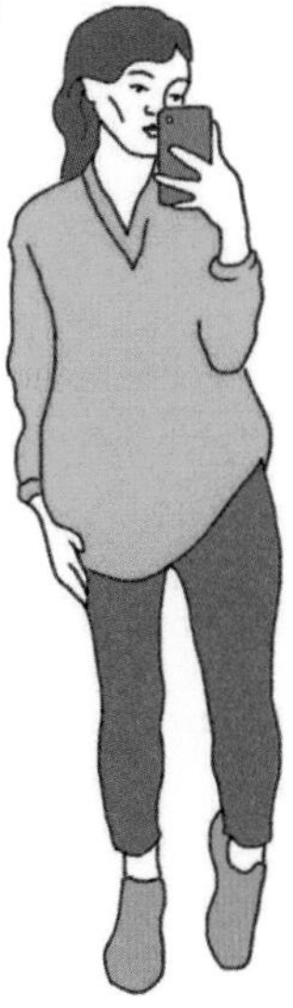

In extreme cases an image of a woman can be used to hold her to ransom. In 2014 the iCloud hacking scandal saw a number of high-profile women face having nude pictures of themselves posted on the internet. American actor Jennifer Lawrence, one of the celebrities the hackers targeted, told the *Hollywood Reporter*'s “Awards Chatter” Podcast in 2017, “I feel like I got gang-banged by the f***ing planet – like, there's not one person in the world that is not capable of seeing these intimate photos of me. You can just be at a barbecue and somebody can just pull them up on their phone. That was a really impossible thing to process.” She went on to describe the experience as “so unbelievably violating that you can't even put it into words”.

The modern celebrity

One American critic who has commented on popular culture and particularly the feminist movement of the past thirty years is **Camille Paglia** (b. 1947). A 2015 essay (again, for the *Hollywood Reporter*) asked, “Can group selfies advance women's goals?” In the piece Paglia uses her typically quick-witted and unsympathetic approach to look at the modern phenomenon of the “girl squad”, made famous by the likes of the American country singer Taylor Swift, who regularly shares pictures of herself and

> *"There's not one person in the world that is not capable of seeing these intimate photos of me [...] That was a really impossible thing to process."*
> Jennifer Lawrence

her celebrity friends, and brings them on stage when she is on tour.

These group selfies (accessorized with the hashtag #squadgoals) have led critics of Swift to suggest that she is using feminism as a marketing tool. Do we blame her, though? "Young women performers are now at the mercy of a swarming, intrusive paparazzi culture, intensified by the hypersexualization of our flesh-baring fashions," says Paglia. "The girl squad phenomenon has certainly been magnified by how isolated and exposed young women feel in negotiating the piranha shoals of the industry."

Making a decision:

These famous women are isolated by a sea of cameras, and we are on the other side of them. Naomi Wolf would tell you this superficiality is a distraction. Something that helps "to airbrush off a woman's face is to erase women's identity, power and history," she says in *The Beauty Myth*. It is a technique that stops you from thinking about what a woman is saying or doing; a technique to undermine women. And at the dawn of the photographic revolution, Susan Sontag saw it coming.

Maybe I'm not as straight as I thought...

Audre Lorde • Jill Johnston • Madonna • Judith Butler

Human sexuality is not easy to categorize. People are waking up to the idea that, perhaps, we don't all fit into boxes. We are slowly beginning to recognize the broad spectrum of sexual desire. The internet is playing a huge role in this. According to recent research conducted at the University of Waterloo in Ontario, Canada, women who consume internet pornography are using new technology to explore their sexuality. They are also using it as a way to connect with others to discuss their sexual interests.

We have focused a lot on gender so far, through the lens of feminist theory, and the roles society plays in forming our expectations of ourselves. But what about sexuality? As the patriarchy has made women "other", so heterosexual love is seen as the standard, while anyone who experiences sexuality in other ways is deemed "other", too. The parallels between the two cannot be understated, and feminists have been investigating this binary division for decades.

One such feminist was **Audre Lorde**, a black lesbian who faced much discrimination for her sexuality. In her 1980 essay "Age, Race, Class and Sex" Lorde recognizes the limiting way in which humanity understands itself as either "man" or "woman"."As a tool of social control, women have been encouraged to recognize only one area of human difference as legitimate, those differences which exist between women and men." She also talked about the need for understanding, and for men and women to accept the fact that they are different, and that there are also a multitude of differences between one woman and another, from one human to the next.

Lorde, who died in 1992, would hopefully be optimistic about the opportunities provided by the internet for making people more accepting and more understanding of how others want and choose to live. Now, you can meet other men and women from around the world who don't fit into the outdated binary, straight version of humanity.

Was that version of humanity ever correct or just a construct of a patriarchal society? Other studies have found that while lesbians are much more attracted to the female form, most women who say they are straight are, in fact, aroused by videos of both naked men and naked women. You might not be the only one asking yourself if you are really as heterosexual as you have grown up to believe.

Are all women lesbians, then?

This was a topic of much debate during the 1960s and 1970s. As referenced in Chapter 3, **Jill Johnston** (1929–2010) was particularly vocal in this area. The prominent American

feminist activist famously said, "All women are lesbians except those that don't know it yet." She also led the separatist movement, which argued that women and men could only be equal if they first learned to live apart from each other. She tied this in – controversially – with sexuality. "Until all women are lesbians there will be no true political revolution," she said in her 1973 book *Lesbian Nation: The Feminist Solution*.

The debate around Johnston's political lesbianism spread across much of the English-speaking world and culminated in the 1981 publication of an infamous booklet, *Love Your Enemy?: The Debate Between Heterosexual Feminism and Political Lesbianism*. In it, a political lesbian was defined as: "a woman-identified woman who does not fuck men. It does not mean compulsory sexual activity with women." It goes on to state, "We think serious feminists have no choice but to abandon heterosexuality. Only in the system of oppression that is male supremacy does the oppressor actually invade and colonize the interior of the body of the oppressed."

This was controversial for many people at the time because of its suggestion that sexual orientation is a matter of choice. A more modern interpretation of sexuality is that it comes from within you. It is an essential part of your being. And so society's attempts to make you think straight love is the only real love is incredibly limiting, and may explain why more and more women are only now finding out that there is more than one dimension to their sexuality.

Madonna, queer theory and refusing to be pigeon-holed

One woman who has refused to be pigeon-holed is global pop megastar **Madonna** (b. 1958). The "Queen of Pop" has had a long and illustrious career, which has flown in the face of the music industry's misogyny and sexism. She has been embroiled in public battles again and again because of her refusal to fit a stereotype, and has evaded definition by turning the tables and experimenting with the different roles given to women.

In her 1990 book, **Judith Butler** (b. 1956), wrote extensively about gender politics *Gender Trouble: Feminism and the Subversion of Identity*, critiquing identity-based politics, claiming that presenting "women" as a coherent group performs "an unwitting regulation and reification of [binary] gender relations". They had very different mediums and audiences – one was a feminist academic and the other a global superstar – but both

> *"All women are lesbians except those that don't know it yet."*
> Jill Johnston

" The master's tools will never dismantle the master's house."

Audre Lorde

Butler and Madonna challenged the narrow constraints of sex and gender. Like Audre Lorde (*see* page 141), Butler wanted the world to accept that there is more than one type of woman, more than men and women, more than straight or gay. She went as far as calling these definitions "chimerical representations of originally heterosexual identities".

But coming out as anything other than the "norm" is not easy for anyone. "I am gay," American poet Maya Angelou (1928–2014) told a gathering of 4,000 mostly LGBT people in 1996. She paused, and continued: "I am lesbian. I am black. I am white. I am Native American. I am Christian. I am Jew. I am Muslim." She believed in the shared humanity of all – regardless of race, gender or religion – and was inviting everyone to embrace their shared humanity, too.

This was not an easy place to inhabit. For Lorde, as one of the first openly black lesbian feminists, life was hard. Her *intersectionality* (*see* page 33) was used against her, and each of the facets of her identity was used against her in some way or another. For instance,

> ## Key consideration
> Does society's binary view of sexuality stop us from ever fully understanding ourselves?

political antagonists tried to discredit her among black students by announcing her sexuality. But this only made her a stronger voice in the feminist movement.

In one moving statement in "Age, Race, Class and Sex" Lorde said: "As a Black lesbian feminist comfortable with the many different ingredients of my identity, and a woman committed to racial and sexual freedom from oppression, I find I am constantly being encouraged to pluck out some one aspect of myself and present this as the meaningful whole, eclipsing or denying the other parts of self. But this is a destructive and fragmenting way to live."

Making a decision:

Lorde denied definition, and instead chose to live through all of her different selves. She would say that trying to fit into someone else's idea of you is a waste of energy, and that people instead need to learn to inhabit all the parts of themselves at once. So embrace your differences. Because being yourself, fully, as many of these women advocate, is the biggest form of rebellion there is.

Why can't I stop buying new clothes?

Betty Friedan • Naomi Wolf • bell hooks

Clothes, throughout history, have represented many things to women. They have meant oppression, strictly guarding your womanhood and dressing you in the image society expects of you, but they have also meant expression, giving you an opportunity to show who you really are through the fabrics you choose or the cut of dress you wear. In most parts of the world you can still observe these two roles side by side.

But no matter where you live, one thing is for sure. It is women who like to shop. According to a 2009 report in the *Harvard Business Review*, globally, women control about $20 trillion in annual consumer spending. That is a lot of spending power. Fashion itself is largely seen as a female pastime and there is a direct pipeline going into it. When American teenagers were asked what their hobbies were in a recent study, the girls said: shopping. In the USA there are more malls than high schools. Go figure.

Fashion is not just a pastime, however. It is big business. The UK has the largest retail and apparel market in Europe, and it is expected to be worth US$77 billion in 2020. No matter where you live in the world, shopping is only getting easier, thanks to the internet. In 2017 the UK had the highest retail e-commerce sales as a percentage of total retail sales (16.9 per cent), followed by China (15.5 per cent), Norway (12.1per cent), Finland (11.2 per cent) and South Korea (11.3 per cent). The US comes in at eight with 8.3 per cent.

When did women become associated with shopping?

Good question. After the Second World War, mass-production meant the consumer-goods market was suddenly big business everywhere. Men returned to their jobs. Women returned to their homes. New methods of industry coincided with some women having more freedom (supposedly) and more time on their hands. And to do what? Shop.

Betty Friedan (1921–2006), the controversial second-wave feminist (*see* page 13), was a particular authority in this field. She published her book *The Feminine*

How did shopping become a woman's prerogative?

> *"Somehow, somewhere, someone must have figured out that women will buy more things if they are kept in the underused, nameless-yearning, energy-to-get-rid-of state of being housewives."*
> Betty Friedan

Mystique in 1963, having seen the explosion of this phenomenon in her home country America. It is important to note, however, that Friedan also came under attack for her brand of feminism, which failed to recognize that many women did not have the luxury of time on their hands, and that for them the situation was worse. They had to work at a job out of the home *as well as* fulfilling their household duties.

But regardless of your level of income, Friedan and others hit on something that affects all women – the stereotypical nature of advertising. The one that purveyed just one American dream: the (white) nuclear family. The husband who went out to work. The woman who stayed at home. The 2.0 children. (*See* also page 88.)

How did brands do this? By telling women that their identity was dictated by what they bought. Feminist Kathy Myers criticized these stereotypes in 1986 in the *Encyclopedia of Feminist Theories*, calling them "dangerously subversive images of women". The rise of consumer culture was tangled up with a singular, idealized version of a woman. She was white, and she worked in the home – and that was where she belonged.

In her 1990 book *The Beauty Myth* **Naomi Wolf** argued that this is because "Consumer culture is best supported by markets made up of sexual clones, men who want objects and women who want to be objects, and the object desired ever-changing, disposable, and

dictated by the market." This transiency, Wolf argued, was to ensure that your dissatisfaction with yourself will grow, rather than diminish, over time. This dissatisfaction is what drives many women to constantly shop.

The relationship between women and advertising

Friedan had similar ideas about how advertisers preyed on women. "Somehow, somewhere, someone must have figured out that women will buy more things if they are kept in the underused, nameless-yearning, energy-to-get-rid-of state of being housewives," she wrote in *The Feminine Mystique*. Again, you can see why she faced criticism here, considering that most women around the world do not ever experience this privileged state of having too much money and not enough to do.

But the women that Friedan talks of specifically are the ones who are targeted by advertisers. The ones susceptible to this, who buy into the idea (quite literally) that they are not good enough without the latest product – be it a dress, an iron or a new brand of moisturizer.

Or, as Friedan puts it: "Dyeing her hair cannot stop time; buying a Plymouth will not give her a new identity; smoking a Marlboro will not get her an invitation to bed, even if that's what she thinks she wants. But those unfulfilled promises can keep her endlessly hungry for things, keep her from ever knowing what she really needs or wants." For Friedan, women are slaves to consumption and this is a form of oppression in itself, keeping you chained to your shopping habit to stop you from realizing that you are empty inside. Sorry.

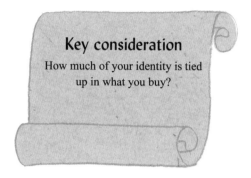

Key consideration

How much of your identity is tied up in what you buy?

Shopping as disease: narcissism and shopaholics

No gentle reprieve now, sadly, as we move on to shopping addictions. The first prominent feminist to address the reasons why women buy and men make was Simone de Beauvoir (1908–86). In a chapter of her 1949 book *The Second Sex*, titled "Narcissism", she explores how women are impotent in the world and therefore must find something to give their life meaning. "Man's truth is in the houses he builds, the forests he clears, the patients he cures," she says, "not being able to accomplish herself in projects and aims, woman attempts to grasp herself in the immanence of her person."

De Beauvoir would certainly be shocked by today's consumer culture. And, sadly, women still seem to be suffering at the sharp end of this. The bored housewife stereotype exists for a reason. It has never been easier for a shopping habit to slide into

addiction and for this narcissism to rear its head on a daily, if not hourly, basis as the fashion cycle speeds up and buying gets increasingly easier.

But the fashion industry isn't just bad for your wallet

Fashion itself has a lot to answer for. It is mistakenly seen as a woman's industry, but if you dig just under the surface, you will find that while women are doing the shopping, it is mainly men who are profiting from it. Some of the most acclaimed fashion houses are owned by international conglomerates, and the creative "wunderkinder" who head up the design departments are almost always men.

"Consumer culture is best supported by markets made up of sexual clones, men who want objects and women who want to be objects, and the object desired ever-changing, disposable, and dictated by the market."
Naomi Wolf

> *"The world of fashion has also come to understand that selling products is heightened by the exploitation of Otherness."*
> bell hooks

The industry does not treat people well, either. There are the underpaid garment workers (primarily women), the maltreated models, the anxiety-inducing advertising and the sexual misconduct. The list goes on.

The other ills plaguing fashion are lack of diversity and *cultural appropriation*. As **bell hooks** (b. 1952) remarks in her 1992 essay "Eating the Other", "The world of fashion has also come to understand that selling products is heightened by the exploitation of Otherness. The success of Benetton ads, which with their racially diverse images have become a model for various advertising strategies, epitomize this trend." Any culture that isn't white is seen as other, seen as something different from the norm. hooks often criticised the way in which white, mainstream culture adopted imagery, symbols and traditions from other cultures and said this only perpetuated the problem of making these cultures "other."

Making a decision:

The stereotype that Friedan hates in *The Feminine Mystique*, the one that imprisons women and makes them – quite literally – slaves to fashion, is still a problem today. And diversity remains a serious issue. Women are sold one singular ideal, and are told again and again that they "must have" this new item and look a certain way to get by in life. It doesn't matter if you are spending your disposable income (and then some) in Gucci or Primark, the message is still the same. Spend money, even if you don't have it: it will make you feel better; it will make you a better person; it will make you a better woman. But will it?

Where are all the women in film?

Geena Davis • Roxane Gay • Laura Mulvey • Virginia Woolf

Since October 2017 the world of film has been alight with scandals. These stories have shone a spotlight on the misconduct that can happen at the hands of the world's elite when too few people share too much power. And this problem is not exclusive to the film industry, as groundbreaking research by actor **Geena Davis** (b. 1956) has discovered.

A woman in film has to defy the odds to continue working after the age of forty. According to research by the Harnisch Foundation and USC Annenberg, only 19.9 per cent of female characters are between the ages of forty and sixty-four. Top-earning female actors take home around 40 per cent of the salaries of their male co-stars. There are success stories, such as Kathryn Bigelow (b. 1951) – in 2009 the first woman to win the Academy Award for best director for *The Hurt Locker* – but they are few and far between, and do not start a movement or change the playing field. The proportion of female directors on the highest-grossing films has fallen since 2001, and only 5 per cent of cinematographers are women.

This problem is universal. Another study by IBM Research India looked at the gender representation of people in Hindi films. A group of researchers used an IBM database of Wikipedia pages of 4,000 movies released between 1970 and 2017, extracting titles, cast information, plots, soundtracks and posters. They also analysed 880 official trailers of movies released between 2008 and 2017.

Over the nearly-fifty-year period, male cast members are mentioned on average thirty times in the film's plot description on Wikipedia compared to female cast members, who are mentioned only 15 times. What do we take from this? We can assume that the actress's role does not bear as much weight as the actor's, so the women have less to say.

This matters. It makes you wonder: why are there so few women in film? Could it have something to do with how they are treated. Could there be some kind of power imbalance here? And could that have something to do with the increasing number of stories around #MeToo (where women share their experiences online or simply

> *"This is the state of affairs for women in entertainment –*
> *everything hangs in the balance all the time."*
> Roxane Gay

acknowledge that they have been victims of sexual misconduct)?

While the allegations against American film producer Harvey Weinstein that emerged in 2017 shone a light on the misdemeanours of multiple people in America's film industry, the problem goes much further. One study conducted in 2017 by the Korean Film Council (KOFIC) and Women in Film Korea found that one in ten women working in film in South Korea – from actors to directors to writers to staff – had experienced "unwanted sexual demands". And why, we ask, are so few women globally sticking it out and making it to the top?

The pressure on the rare female-led movie

On the rare occasion that a female-led or female-directed series or film does get the greenlight, it becomes subject to enormous amounts of criticism. For example, the American TV series *Girls* (2012–17) and the 2011 film *Bridesmaids* both found themselves criticized and pulled apart in a way that the staggering number of other TV shows and films that don't have women at the forefront don't. **Roxane Gay** (b. 1974), author of the 2014 book *Bad Feminist*, says this is because they are so unusual. These women are truly doing something different and for that they are punished.

"There was a lot of pressure on that movie," says Gay of *Bridesmaids*. "[It] had to be good if any other women-driven comedies had any hope of being produced. This is the state of affairs for women in entertainment – everything hangs in the balance all the time." Gay often addresses the problem of lack of roles for women in film at the same time as addressing the lack of diversity. For her, the two are part of the same problem.

Started by activist Tarana Burke in 2006, the #metoo movement gained widespread fame in 2017.

The camera and the male gaze

Laura Mulvey (b. 1941) is another woman who has weighed in on this debate, this time from a film theory angle. Mulvey is best known for her essay "Visual Pleasure and Narrative Cinema", published in 1975 in the British film theory journal *Screen*. Mulvey argues that the only way to get rid of the patriarchal Hollywood system is to radically challenge and reshape the strategies of classical Hollywood with alternative feminist methods. A good starting point could be to encourage the creation of films from outside traditional studio routes; independent films from around the world often work to challenge the stereotypes that many big-budget Hollywood movies perpetuate.

Mulvey specifically points out that often in cinema women are depicted in a passive role. "In their traditional exhibitionist role women are simultaneously looked at and displayed, with their appearance coded for strong visual and erotic impact so that they can be said to connote *to-be-looked-at-ness*," she writes. For Mulvey, if women are ever to be equally represented in the workplace, or anywhere, they must be portrayed as men are: as lacking sexual objectification.

A scene of one's own

But this problem is not just about sexual objectification, as English author **Virginia Woolf** (1882–1941) pointed out nearly a century ago. In *A Room of One's Own* (1928) she recognized how often women were portrayed by men, and how narrow that portrayal was. "They are now and then mothers and daughters," she writes. "But almost without exception they are shown in their relation to men. It was strange to think that all the great women of fiction were,

> **Key consideration**
>
> If you can't see yourself in the mainstream media, how much does that limit your expectations of yourself?

until Jane Austen's day, not only seen by the other sex, but seen only in relation to the other sex. And how small a part of a woman's life is that."

Woolf was said, in turn, to have inspired another movement within modern cinema, the Bechdel Test, named after the American cartoonist Alison Bechdel (b. 1960). In order to pass the Bechdel Test, a film has to include a scene where two women talk to each other about something other than a man. It is staggering how few films pass the test.

The 17 per cent rule

Why is this important? Because of the amount of media we consume. Children, in particular, are engaging with media up to seven hours a day. That is what led *Thelma & Louise* actor Geena Davis to set up an institution to promote gender equality and diversity, with a special branch called See Jane, whose tagline is: "If she can see it, she can be it."

Women and girls are 51 per cent of the population, and yet entertainment media is consistently bereft of female representation

> *"If she can see it, she can be it."*
> See Jane

on screen. From a young age, girls are being taught that they are less important. In research done by Davis and her team over a twenty-year period, they found that for every female speaking character there were three males, while female characters made up just 17 per cent of crowd scenes.

In fact, the ratio of male-to-female characters has been exactly the same since 1946. "As with wider society, part of the problem lies in the fact that the key decision-makers remain overwhelmingly white, male and middle-aged," observed Davis.

Not convinced that the films we watch can influence our behaviour? See Jane quotes one particular incident that highlights the need for this to change. In 2012 the sport of archery became suddenly popular among girls, at the same time as two movies starring female heroines as archers were released: *The Hunger Games* and *Brave*. In a study by the Geena Davis Institute on Gender in Media that examined this, seven out of ten girls said that they had taken up the sport because they were inspired by either Katniss or Merida.

Is it getting better?

Thanks to initiatives such as Geena Davis's and others, the situation for women in film is getting better. American actors Reese Witherspoon (b. 1976) and Sandra Bullock (b. 1964) have both set up very successful production companies that commission more female-led, female-directed stories, and Angelina Jolie (b. 1975) is increasingly creating her own material to star in.

Male actors are helping to change the scene, too. Hoping to exercise his own influence in a positive manner, Bollywood actor and filmmaker Farhan Akhtar (b. 1974) set up Men Against Rape and Discrimination (MARD), a social campaign he launched in India "to make people think more positively", to empower women in India and to highlight the need for gender equality.

The Time's Up campaign, set up in 2018 by 300 women who work in film, television and theatre to protest against gender inequality and harassment in the workplace, is another initiative hoping to make a difference.

Making a decision:

But what else needs to change in order to level the playing field? For women to have more roles, men need to accept roles where they aren't the lead, and accept lower pay to redress the balance. This all helps toward creating an entertainment industry that gives everyone the media that they want and deserve.

Why do we need women's magazines?

Audre Lorde • Barbara Smith • Gloria Steinem • Virginia Woolf • Naomi Wolf • JINHA

From the women's section of a newspaper to a glossy magazine to a publishing imprint commissioning only women's work, the media landscape is full of content aimed directly at women. But why do we need articles, books and stories published in this way? Why does it matter if we have these women-only spaces or not? The answer to that lies in the thinking of some of the 20th century's greatest feminists, and in the exciting new media landscape of today.

Where do we start? Well, the media landscape is fickle and change happens quickly. During moments of great social change the newspapers and magazines we consume adapt to meet demand. Newspapers need to sell in order to make money and to keep advertisers, so it is not surprising that more often than not editors find themselves walking a tightrope between what people want to read and pushing other agendas (their own or, most likely, those of their advertisers).

During feminism's second wave (*see* page 13) a host of new publications and imprints sprang up to address the topic of the day: equality. *Cosmopolitan* was given a post-war makeover to meet the requirements of a more liberated female audience, while new ventures such as *Spare Rib* magazine, book publisher Virago and, later, *Ms.* magazine and Kitchen Table: Women of Color Press (*see* page 154) pushed the media industry into new directions and, for the first time, gave women a unique opportunity to speak from a platform that was not edited by men. (Although, ironically, when the UK's BBC first aired its women-only show *Woman's*

Hour in 1946, it was presented by none other than a male broadcaster.) But change was certainly happening, albeit slowly.

Virago is one of the most famous women's imprints. Launched in 1973, it described itself as "the first mass-market publisher for 52% of the population – women. An exciting new imprint for both sexes in a changing world." Virago's first book was *Fenwomen* by Mary Chamberlain, and the publishing company inscribed on all of its later books a quote by Sheila Rowbotham from her 1972 book *Women, Resistance and Revolution:* "It is only when women start to organize in large numbers that we become a political force, and begin to move toward the possibility of a truly democratic society in which every human being can be brave, responsible, thinking and diligent in the struggle to live at once freely and unselfishly."

Giving voices to marginalized women

In 1980 **Audre Lorde** (1934–92) and **Barbara Smith** (b. 1946) founded another type of publishing company. It was called Kitchen Table: Women of Color Press,

and was dedicated entirely to furthering the writings of black feminists. The group wanted to do something "radical": print books that were aimed at promoting the writing of women of colour of all racial/ethnic heritages, national origins, ages, socioeconomic classes and sexual orientations.

This was a major moment. Kitchen Table was the first publishing company run, completely autonomously, by women of colour. Women – and particularly marginalized women – were not being catered for as an audience or as creators and purveyors of culture. The mass media of the time did not make space for these women – and so they had to make their own.

In her essay "A Press of our Own. Kitchen Table: Women of Color Press", founder Barbara Smith described the early days of the business: "In October 1980, Audre Lorde said to me during a phone conversation, 'We really need to do something about publishing.'" Smith goes on to talk about why marginalized women needed their own platform so much. "Why were we so strongly motivated to attempt the impossible?" she asks. "An early slogan of the women in print movement was 'freedom of the press belongs to those who own the press'. This is even truer for multiple disenfranchised women of color who have minimal access to power, including the power of media, except what we wrest from an unwilling system."

Perhaps most tellingly, Smith points out that

> *"It is only when women start to organize in large numbers that we become a political force, and begin to move towards the possibility of a truly democratic society in which every human being can be brave, responsible, thinking and diligent in the struggle to live at once freely and unselfishly."*
> Sheila Rowbotham

as feminists and lesbian writers of colour, they knew they would only get published "at the mercy or whim of others – in either commercial or alternative publishing, since both are white dominated". This highlighted the major issue that existed within the women's movement of the time: race. With many white, straight women such as **Gloria Steinem** (b. 1934) being given increasing amounts of airtime by the national and international media, women of other backgrounds and identities were beginning to feel like the movement was not for them, emphasizing further how much they needed space to tell their own stories.

So where is the "men's" section?

Any eagle-eyed newspaper reader may have asked themselves: why is there a section of this newspaper/website aimed directly at women? Where is the bit just for men? Maybe the whole thing is aimed at men? While we wait for gender equality to be a reality, we still need spaces for women to talk to other women (although perhaps men could do with educating themselves a bit better on what are deemed to be exclusively "women's" issues).

Virginia Woolf, who often spoke about the need for these sorts of places, said in her prototypical feminist text *A Room of One's Own* (1928), "Women are alone, unlit by the capricious and coloured light of the other sex." Throughout history, women have been seen through men's eyes. Since around 1970, however, that has begun to change.

> # Key consideration
> Will true equality mean there is no need for women to have designated spaces in which to communicate with each other freely?

Women have had a chance to speak for themselves, to show themselves and even to view themselves in a way that is not defined by men.

In a different but relevant vein, in *The Beauty Myth* (1990) **Naomi Wolf** reflects on the strange relationship that women have with their modern media diet. Why do you care what female celebrities are wearing, or let someone tell you what clothes you should be buying? "They care because, though the magazines are trivialized, they represent something very important: women's mass culture," suggests Wolf. "A woman's magazine is not just a magazine. The relationship between the woman reader and her magazine is so different from that between a man and his that they aren't in the same category."

Do women have opinions?

A 2017 study by the Women's Media Center (WMC) – which was co-founded by Gloria Steinem, actor Jane Fonda (b. 1937) and writer Robin Morgan (b. 1941) – found

155

> *"Though the magazines are trivialized, they represent something very important: women's mass culture. A woman's magazine is not just a magazine."*
> Naomi Wolf

that at the three big American television networks, ABC, CBS and NBC combined, men report three times as much of the news as women do. Work by women anchors, field reporters and correspondents has actually declined, falling to 25.2 per cent of

62%

38%

In the US media (including Internet, TV, print etc.), men receive 62% of credits and bylines.

Source: Women's Media Center, 2017

reports in 2016 from 32 per cent when the organization published its previous report in 2015. Apparently, opinions are a male thing.

From the USA to Turkey, women all over the world are still fighting for their right to speak and be heard. The news agenda is largely driven by news agencies, which connect the world and sell their stories directly to publishers.

Recently in Turkey a Kurdish all-female news agency called **JINHA** was set up to redress the balance during the systemic silencing of dissenting voices. It was shut down in 2016, but it is a valiant example of why women need their own spaces to tell their own stories. Because often, they are not wanted. And like the women behind Kitchen Table, the women of JINHA decided to take matters into their own hands.

Making a decision:

The needs of women are not universal and they change with the times. From Virginia Woolf to Naomi Wolf, from a revolutionary publishing company for women of colour to a Kurdish all-women news agency, everyone with a voice needs somewhere to exercise it. And these examples all show one thing: women need their own spaces in order to push for real change

Is technology sexist?

Sadie Plant • Donna Haraway • Cibelle Cavalli Bastos • Mary Wollstonecraft • Laurie Penny

Have you noticed how the media we consume affects us? As human life continues to change at an increasing speed, we have another thing to think about: how the technology we are creating is affecting our human experience, and what that technology says about us. This is no longer a question of what we watch on TV, but how the devices and software we use all day are shaping the world around us. For better, or for worse?

When Apple released an iPhone with a full health suite, minus any mention of periods – which, as you know, affect half the global population – it received a fair bit of criticism. Where were the women making the decisions about what the health app should include? This one incident spoke volumes about the lack of women in technology, and shone a spotlight on the importance of having women in tech.

Because right now, men are building the future – and this is creating all sorts of other problems. From sexual misconduct, to the stereotype of the "brogrammer", to the lack of women in Silicon Valley boardrooms, the tech industry is shutting women out.

And women are set to lose out because of tech in other ways, too, according to the "Future of Jobs" report released in 2016 by the World Economic Forum. "The Industry Gender Gap: Women and Work in the Fourth Industrial Revolution" reports that women all over the world could end up fighting for equality and jobs not just with men, but also with robots – in the form of artificially intelligent machines.

The cyberfeminists offered a solution – a long time ago

Back in the 1990s, technology posed as many answers as questions. For example, could cyborgs be used to transcend gender? Tech offered an alternative to the stereotypes and issues that plague society. The cyberfeminists hoped to use it to challenge stereotypes, rather than perpetuate them.

And yet, the opposite has happened. Think of a robot, for example, which helps you order your groceries when you get home from work and asks you if you have had a good day. Does the robot you think of sound like a man or a woman? If you answered "woman", it is hardly surprising. Think of

"By the late 20th century, our time, a mythic time, we are all chimeras, theorized and fabricated hybrids of machine and organism; in short, we are all cyborgs."
Donna Haraway

157

> *"The system adapts, and we can rewrite it so it works better – or we can make it a playroom for the prejudices of the past. It's up to us."*
> Laurie Penny

all the useful tech you use that does have a woman's voice. Alexa, for instance. Maybe your Satnav. The voice at the end of the phone when you call an automated call centre. More often than not, it is a woman helping you feel calm and relaxed, being subservient to you.

The cyberfeminists did not envisage the world this way. The word itself was originally coined in 1994 by the British philosopher **Sadie Plant** (b. 1964) – once described in the *Independent on Sunday* as the "IT girl for the 21st century".

One of the most prominent thinkers who shaped the movement, though, was **Donna Haraway** (b. 1944). In her iconic 1985 essay "A Cyborg Manifesto: Science, Technology, and Socialist-Feminism in the Late Twentieth Century" (*see* quote, page 157), the post-humanist scholar and feminist theorist addressed the issues of gender "norms", imagined the future of feminism and proposed the cyborg as the answer to mankind's problems. Part-human and part-machine, the cyborg she imagined would

challenge racial and patriarchal biases. "This," Haraway wrote, "is the self [that] feminists must code." Haraway's vision of the future has still not materialized. Coding the self has been left almost entirely to men. And while the tech we use has matured, the hope that it might provide some kind of intersectional feminist utopia has not been realized.

Assigning gender to robots

This is not something to simply feel nostalgic about, but something to work against. From Twitter to porn sites, the internet has become an echo chamber where users seek out communities that reflect their offline opinions. "Networked knowledge," wrote David Weinberger (b. 1950) in a 2016 essay "Rethinking Knowledge in the Internet Age" in the *Los Angeles Review of Books*, "is inextricable from its social context." The networks the internet has created are new platforms built on old ideas.

Artist **Cibelle Cavalli Bastos** (b. 1978) uses "malware" as a metaphor for our prejudices. "We function like some sort of computer that ends up getting a lot of malware installed without realizing," she said at the ICA's Post-Cyber Feminist International Conference in 2017. "Racism, sexism, classism: that's all malware. We learn that shit and we need to get it out of our system. We need to deprogram."

Think about how this works with robots. The robots we build, like the networks we have created, are not inextricable from

Key consideration
Are we projecting our own stereotypes – and cementing them into the future – through the technology we're building?

social context, either. Which is why it is problematic when we assign genders to robots. A robot could be given a "female" voice to make it sound helpful and nurturing, while a "male" robot was designed to be more authoritative.

This gets only more problematic when you consider the repercussions of people owning "sex robots". In some sort of gothic prediction **Mary Wollstonecraft** (1759–97) described in her 1792 book *A Vindication of the Rights of Women* what a man expects a woman to be: "She was created to be the toy of man, his rattle, and it must jingle in his ears whenever, dismissing reason, he chooses to be amused." What difference is there between the woman Wollstonecraft describes

here and the sex robot a man buys for his own amusement?

What's the difference between women and robots?

Here, we turn again to **Laurie Penny**, in the context of the increasingly popular "man meets bot, man falls in love with bot" dystopian narrative. From *Metropolis* (1927) to *Ex Machina* (2014), we see the same story repeated: "The protagonist [...] goes through agonies trying to work out whether his silicon sweetheart is truly sentient," observes Penny in a 2016 article for the *New Statesman*. "If she is, is it right for him to exploit her [...]? If she isn't, can he can truly fall in love with her?" She goes on to ask: "Does it matter? And [...] will she rebel, and how can she be stopped?" These are questions that society has been asking for centuries about not robots, but women. As the technology we use increasingly becomes a part of everyday life, consider how this is shaping the world, because these alternate realities we create do have an effect on our own reality.

Making a decision:

So is technology sexist? Yes, because men and women (but largely men) with their own built-in biases have made it. And from porn to video games to subservient robots, the media we consume and the technology we live with teaches us about the world around us. As Penny says in *Cybersexism: Sex, Gender and Power on the Internet* (*see* quote, opposite), "...we can rewrite it so it works better...It's up to us."

It's My Body

Chapter 6

Why do I always feel fat?

Emily Edwards • Susie Orbach • Naomi Wolf

In her lecture at the 2007 Perspectives on Power conference, "Are Eating Disorders Feminist? Power, Resistance, and the Feminine Ideal", historian **Emily Edwards** started by addressing the state of play today. One of the major components of beauty in our society, she said, is thinness. Within Western culture, the importance of women being thin has steadily increased. In fact, she noted, "thinness" has become ingrained in women's heads as being synonymous with "femininity", and representative of success, intelligence and willpower.

Edwards carried out a study of 40 women who had recovered from eating disorders. She found that they had thoroughly internalized the idea that their lives would be better if they were thinner – echoing the findings of British psychotherapist **Susie Orbach** (b. 1946) when she was writing *Fat Is a Feminist Issue* in 1978.

Orbach and Edwards stress that women are under constant bombardment from the media to lose weight, in magazine and newspaper articles and advertisements, online and on TV. Images of "perfect" women run side by side with these articles, suggesting that if women just "worked on" their bodies more, they, too, could look like this.

Impossibly perfect

As Orbach and others have pointed out, this is a commercially winning concept for the dieting, exercise, makeup and cosmetic surgery industries. In 2017 the dieting and weight-loss industry was estimated to be worth over $60 billion in the USA alone. In putting forward an unattainable "ideal" these industries can expect ever increasing profits. Even the models shown do not look like that in real life; their images are routinely digitally altered to make their bodies into the "perfect" shape. And this, despite such pressure on models to be so "abnormally thin" that, according to Kirstie Clements, former editor of *Vogue Australia*, many have taken to eating paper tissue, rather than food, to quell their hunger. Some starve themselves for several days at a time, she said, and often become so weak that they struggle to keep their eyes open and have to be hospitalized. Yet even their extremely thin bodies are digitally reshaped before publication to more closely resemble Western culture's idea of a "beautiful woman".

Globalization might have led to a vast number of ways in which women could be considered beautiful, Orbach notes. Instead, however, it has not only narrowed down the ideal to one particular type, but it has also led to this stereotype being used and accepted worldwide. Today even the women of Fiji and Tokyo are chasing the same long-legged, large breasted, tiny-waisted body as their Western counterparts.

> *"Dieting is the most potent political sedative in women's history; a quietly mad population is a tractable one."*
> Naomi Wolf

Why do women care about models?

Before women were able to work in the public arena in (reasonably) well-paid jobs, they relied on their fathers or husbands to support them. Orbach suggests that many heterosexual women still believe that their future involves finding a male partner to live with (perhaps marry) and have a child. "Getting a man", she said, is presented as an almost-unattainable but also essential goal. There is an element of panic attached. Women are told in various ways that they are competing against each other for this rare but essential resource, so they need both to get ahead in the beauty stakes and to demean other women, especially regarding any slip-ups in their beauty routine. Every woman, says Orbach, is encouraged to start seeing herself as an object, which can become the focus of a self-improvement project. It is a project that necessarily lasts her lifetime, because no woman will ever reach the digital "ideal", so she will feel forever lacking – in looks, desirability, determination and control (hence the link to success, intelligence and willpower mentioned by Edwards). Her self-esteem and confidence will plummet because, as Edwards noted, "femininity itself" has become tied to this ideal. If you fail to be thin, you fail to be feminine and you fail to be desirable – and so you feel worthless. And that, says **Naomi Wolf**, in her 1990 book *The Beauty Myth*, is the point.

"Femininity", Wolf asserts, is a key word that should always alert women to the fact that they are being pointed toward an idea of womanhood that is presented as "natural", while actually being entirely constructed by men. The ideas of femininity over the centuries have changed, not because of the vagaries of fashion, but as a backlash response to women's surges of independence. We are being spun a beauty myth that is nothing less than a "political weapon against women's advancement", according to Wolf. Patriarchy needs to find ways to keep women "in their place" in very particular ways, not least because capitalism depends upon the free and underpaid labour of women in the home and elsewhere but does not wish to openly acknowledge this, despite the efforts of economists during the 20th century to bring this labour into the general picture (*see* page 80). Wolf quotes John Kenneth Galbraith (1908–2006), a celebrated Canadian-born economist, as noting that women are also "essential to the development of our industrial society" as consumers. Galbraith claimed that it is for economic reasons that there is a "persistence of the view of homemaking as a 'higher calling'...behaviour that is essential for economic reasons is transformed into a social virtue".

Wolf is suggesting that capitalism and patriarchy are working hand in hand here, to produce consumers, cheap labour and unpaid support of paid male workers at home. A changing idea of "femininity" is the tool used to keep control of women; to make them think that everything the patriarchal capitalist system wants from them is "natural", when in fact it is a form of "social coercion". The beauty myth, Wolf says, "is not about women at all. It is about men's institutions and institutional power."

Patriarchal power was not threatened by women until countries began to industrialize; until then, all institutions – governments, businesses, religions, cultural and educational institutions – were run by men in a way that was unopposed. But with the Industrial Revolution, from the mid-18th to the mid-19th century, women started to move into the public arena. Previously they had worked in homes – their own and others' – both unpaid and paid (taking in laundry and piecework), but now they began to seek work outside the home, and then began demanding a vote.

Key consideration
Who has decided what "beauty" looks like?

Independence and body image

It is no coincidence, Wolf says, that women in countries around the world began pressing for (and winning) the right to vote around 1920, and the cultural idea that they should become thinner was born at the same time. Wolf points to the work of the feminist fashion historian Anne Hollander (1940–2014), who found that the idea of beauty before this was very different. In the 15th to 17th century "beautiful" women portrayed in art had "big, ripe bellies", and in the 18th and 19th centuries they had "plump faces and shoulders". They looked healthy and strong. However, between 1918 and 1925 "the rapidity with which the new, linear form replaced the more curvaceous one is startling", Hollander notes. Suddenly, visual portrayals of women had "the look of

Women have been told that they must constantly try to "improve" themselves.

sickness, the look of poverty, and the look of nervous exhaustion".

Each time women have gained a little more power – getting jobs, money, independence – the patriarchal system has to find a way to take that feeling of power away from them, Wolf contends. It does this through challenging women to check they are really "feminine". The way it posed this question throughout the 19th and early 20th centuries was through myths of motherhood, domesticity, chastity and passivity.

During the 1950s women who had enjoyed working in the public arena in the 1940s were pulled back into the home (freeing up jobs for men returning from the Second World War) by the cult of domesticity, from which, according to Wolf, they were later awakened by Betty Friedan (*see* page 102). It is notable, Wolf says, that during that time, when women were safely back in their place, the grip of men's control on women's size loosened, and women were allowed to be curvier, without being ridiculed. But as

women saw through the myth of domesticity and repeated their demands for fuller lives, returning to "the male spheres, en masse", an "urgent social expedient" overrode men's delight in women's curvier bodies. The beauty myth developed to fulfil the coercive function that domesticity had previously performed. This was a really insidious move, Wolf says, because in using this myth, the prison became internalized. Where women were once locked in the "prisons" of their homes, now they are locked in the prisons of their own bodies, attempting to constantly attend to them, evaluate them and change them in a never-ending way that seeks to attain a completely unattainable goal. "Inexhaustible but ephemeral beauty took over from inexhaustible but ephemeral housework," says Wolf.

Thinness plays such an important part in the beauty myth, Wolf asserts, because it takes up so much of women's attention and time (leaving men to other things), and constantly reminds them that their worth

depends on their desirability, which in turn depends on their proximity to the "ideal" beauty (constructed by men, who will then judge their desirability and "worth"). It sets them in competition against one another for the resource that is men, which they are told they need (and that in having one, they will have proved their worth to other men and women); and, she notes, "it keeps them quiet". Wolf quotes the work of researchers J Polivy and C P Herman, who found that both prolonged and periodic caloric restriction leads to passivity, anxiety and emotionality. These three traits, says Wolf, are what "the dominant culture wants to create in the private sense of self of recently liberated women in order to cancel out the dangers of their liberation."

Feminist waves make women feel like they are worth more than their surrounding cultures tell them, and they push for greater freedom. But patriarchal capitalism depends on them to function as unpaid and low-paid labour, so women must be convinced that they are worth less, not more. The beauty myth acts to tell women that unless they are *that* beautiful, and *that* thin, they are not really worth very much. They need to go and work on improving themselves. This is the backlash, says Wolf. The idea that you should strive forever to be thinner, prettier and shorn of "unwanted hair", and all the other distracting, expensive, time-consuming ideas, are actually to stave off your threat to the patriarchy.

Making a decision:

Being fat may be a form of rebellion, Orbach says in *Fat Is a Feminist Issue*. "My fat says 'screw you' to all who want me to be the perfect mom, sweetheart, maid and whore. Take me for who I am, not for who I'm supposed to be." Wolf says that we need to remember that we are being spun a myth that is leaving us spellbound for reasons to do with economics and social control. "The beauty myth is not, ultimately, about appearance or dieting or surgery or cosmetics," she says. It "could not care less how much women weigh…If we were all to go home tomorrow and say we never meant it really – we'll do without the jobs, the autonomy, the orgasms, the money – the beauty myth would slacken at once and grow more comfortable." But while women demand freedom, the beauty myth will continue to tighten around them. And you will always feel fat, no matter what you weigh.

If men could have babies, would everything change?

Gerda Lerner • Karin van Nieuwkerk • Alison Boden • Janice Delaney
Mary Jane Lupton • Emily Toth

According to the historian **Gerda Lerner** (1920–2013), worship of the great goddesses in the early Middle East celebrated the sacredness of female sexuality and woman's incredible ability to create a child. Women were revered as powerful beings. Unfortunately, it was all downhill for women from then on, with the growth of religions that suggested women's reproductive system means they are locked forever into a physicality that prevents them from being spiritual (or intellectual or rational).

It sometimes seems as though men can't really decide whether women are frighteningly powerful or incredibly weak and not worthy of notice. Even the world's largest religions have wrestled with this problem, as they tend to feature powerful mother figures but deny earthly women any actual power within the institutional hierarchies. The Hindu pantheon recognizes goddesses of both forms: there are nurturing divinities, such as Parvati and Sita, but also terrifying ones, including Kali, who wears a garland of skulls and a skirt of dismembered arms. Kali is often depicted standing on the body of Shiva, whom she seems to be trampling to death (an image that has something of the stereotype of a "feminist" about it). Here, we have woman "revealed" as a powerful and man-killing thing, if she is given full reign, justifying the need to socialize her into docility (and not allow her mind to fill with dangerous feminist ideas). Hindu scholars may patiently explain that the goddess Kali represents the need

to kill the ego, that in stories she kills only demons and that in standing on Shiva she is metaphorically contrasting "form", or body, with Shiva's "formless awareness". However, those scholarly comments have largely been lost on Western commentators, who take one look at her terrifying embodiment and declare her to be representative of death, sexuality and violence (an idea that was still perpetuated through authoritative texts such as the *Encyclopaedia Britannica* in 2017).

Kali is a useful figure for understanding how bodies play a role in power dynamics, because she may represent male fears about female power, but she also represents "the body", while Shiva, under her feet, represents "awareness" or spirituality. The idea that men are thinking, intellectual beings while women are mired in the body was to play a central part in most religions. In Christianity, for example, men are seen as being above women in the hierarchy because men are spiritual beings, and therefore closer to God, while women – who remain rooted in the flesh through menstruation and childbirth – are closer to animals. Simply by inhabiting a female body, women are "less than" men in religious terms, and this can never change. In 1995 the Pope explained that he was helpless to allow women to become priests in the Catholic Church because "the presence of a certain diversity of roles is in no way prejudicial to women, provided that this diversity is not the result of an arbitrary imposition, but is rather an expression of what is specific to being male and female". That "specific" thing is the female body.

Within Islamic culture, a woman's body – with its necessary reproductive parts – has traditionally been seen as so alluring that it must be covered up. As anthropologist and religious expert **Karin van Nieuwkerk** argues within this perspective, "whatever women do, they are first and foremost perceived as enticing bodies" (Nieuwkerk, 1988). The male body is seen as having several dimensions (able to operate within the economic or political fields, for example) whereas women, "even if they do not move and dance, but simply walk or work in the male space, are perceived as sexual beings".

Within Islam, the stereotype of women's being is so entrenched within "the body" and sexuality that men are thought to be in danger of losing their self-control, according to **Alison Boden**, Dean of Religious Life at Princeton University. She claims that this

The goddess Kali standing on top of Shiva.

remains true even though the 1981 Universal Islamic Declaration of Human Rights (UIDHR) states that all persons have equal human value.

The solution to women's allure (and assumed capacity to distract men from higher pursuits) has been – at various times and in various places – to exclude women from the sphere of men, both in the workplace and the home. Boden points out that this was as true in Renaissance Italy as in other countries today. Likewise, the veil – so often associated with Islam today – originated from ancient Indo-European cultures, such as the Greeks, Romans and Persians. Urban women in Western Europe during the Middle Ages dressed in clothes that covered them entirely,

"Women's regular bleeding engenders phantoms."
Paracelsus, 16th century Swiss physician

apart from the face, in a form that is echoed in the burka of today, and it became part of the classic Western nun's way of dressing.

Cursed by their bodies

Throughout the course of history, the female body has proved problematic for men of all countries and beliefs. Reflecting the paradox of being seen as both too powerful and too weak, it is viewed as both too seductive and too disgusting. This can be seen particularly in the taboo that still surrounds menstruation in every country today. "Go apart from women during the monthly course, do not approach them until they are clean," advises the Quran (2:222), while in the Bible we are told, "in her menstrual impurity, she is unclean…Likewise, whoever touches them shall be unclean and shall wash his clothes and bathe in water and be unclean until evening," (Leviticus 15). The first Latin

Now commonly associated with Islam, the veil was once worn by Western women in the Middle Ages, and is still worn by Western nuns.

encyclopedia, in 73 AD, claimed that contact with menstrual blood "turns new wine sour, crops touched by it become barren, grafts die, seed in gardens are dried up, the fruit of trees fall off, the edge of steel and the gleam of ivory are dulled, hives of bees die, even bronze and iron are at once seized by rust". Hold on, women are probably exclaiming, it is not that bad! How did it come to take such a violent hold of the male imagination?

In the 1976 feminist text *The Curse: A Cultural History of Menstruation*, sociologists **Janice Delaney**, **Mary Jane Lupton** and **Emily Toth** explored the taboo surrounding menstruation. They discovered the "father of Western science", Aristotle, confirmed men's superiority by declaring that their role in reproduction was the "active matter" (sperm) while women's was passive. Women didn't seem to produce anything during sex, so it was assumed that semen was an active, productive substance. Women's menstrual blood, on the other hand, was associated with miscarriage and the lack of life, so it was viewed as "degenerative" and signifying a kind of passivity that moved toward death. (This is one possible starting place for those tenacious myths that "men are active and productive, while women are passive and don't contribute anything".)

Before long, the uterus became the focus of attention as the cause of women's weakness and uselessness. The Persian physician and philosopher Ibn Sina (known as Avicenna in the West, c. 980–1037) said that "the uterus is the weak point of the female", and by the 18th century the English physician John

> *"Be not ashamed women... You are the gates of the body, and you are the gates of the soul."*
> Walt Whitman

Freind (1675–1728) had linked menstrual blood to hysteria. If men produced that much blood, his reasoning went, they too would be "hysterical". A new idea took hold: women's propensity to bleed was the cause of not only weakness but also mental disorder. Women are, by virtue of their bodies, naturally hysterical (this idea rumbled all the way to Freud and led to the founding of psychoanalysis).

One of the long-term effects of men's theories from past times regarding female reproductive organs is that many women came to believe that they were true. Not, perhaps, that menstrual blood could cause fruit to drop from the trees, but that it was strictly taboo and should not be talked about, even among other women. Campaigners fighting "period poverty" around the world are arguing that the taboo around menstruation is now costing girls their education, as girls unable to buy expensive sanitary products tend to absent themselves from school, rather than try to cope with

Key consideration

If men were to have babies, would the economic advantage switch genders?

a mixture of rags, newspapers and plastic bags, and the danger of blood seeping onto clothing. Girls were facing this situation in every country of the world in 2017; only the governments of India and Kenya began to address it by providing free menstrual products in schools. Elsewhere, the problem is being "tastefully" ignored, and girls unable to afford sanitary products are penalized for "truanting" while menstruating, both at school and in their inability to achieve academically over the long term.

Making a decision:

Gloria Steinem said, "Patriarchy – or whatever you want to call it, the systems that say there's masculine and feminine and other bullshit – is about controlling reproduction. Every economics course ought to start not with production but with reproduction." Writer Angela Carter spelled it out more fully, saying, "If men could have babies, they would cease to be men as such. They would become the 'other'."

Do I really need to go bare down there?

Christine Hope • Merran Toerien • Sue Wilkinson • Andrea Dworkin • Gail Dines

Feminists are always curious about the formation of new cultural norms, and the introduction of the triple-X, or full Brazilian wax, in the late 1980s prompted a renewal of research into women's treatment of their own bodies and the potential links to media portrayals – in this case, pornography. Until around 1990 the major men's magazines showed models with public hair, but this disappeared almost completely after the year 2000. Was there a link?

In 1982 feminist researcher **Christine Hope** investigated the development of female hair removal in her article "Caucasian Female Body Hair and American Culture". She suggested it is the everyday customs that are most "taken for granted" that may be most useful in helping us to understand a particular culture, so this subject merits attention. She found that women did not remove hair from their underarms or legs before the First World War, but by 1945 it was common practice. The three great "periods of hair removal" that she discovered (The Great Underarm Campaign, 1915–19; Coming to Terms with Leg Hair, 1920–40; and A Minor Assault on Leg Hair, 1941–5) coincided with eras in which women made significant gains politically and economically. They got the vote, entered the public world of work and cast off their restrictive clothing. In acting to accentuate "difference" between men and women, "smooth skin" helps to place men more firmly in opposition to women, Hope suggested; so as a cultural practice hair removal demands an increase in "femininity" and a move away from the male

sphere, whenever it is in danger of being invaded. New hair-removal practices (such as the Brazilian) signal a cultural backlash against feminist gains.

Hope suggested that the move toward hair removal in the early 20th century was linked to the American concern with cleanliness, but also seemed to reflect "American beliefs about sex roles". There are two things at play here, she suggested. First, traits defined as "masculine" – such as independence, aggressiveness, objectivity – are automatically defined as "unfeminine", and vice versa. In seeking to remain "feminine", women inadvertently deny these traits in themselves. Second, there is a tendency "to think of adults as male and to lump women with non-adults". She pointed to an experiment in which people were asked to specify the traits of three types of mature, socially competent adults: a man, a woman and an gender-unspecified adult. The list of traits identified as male and adult were very similar, including characteristics such as "very dominant", "very objective" and "not at all easily influenced". The traits associated with adult females, on the other hand, included "very submissive", "very subjective" and "very easily influenced". Hope and the experimenters concluded that this puts women in a conflictual position: do they choose to exhibit the positive traits considered desirable in men and adults, but have their femininity questioned (that is, be a "deviant" woman (*see* page 112), or do they "behave in the prescribed feminine manner, accept a second-class status, and possibly live a lie"?

Hope notes that in being told they should rid themselves of body hair, women are being asked to "get rid of certain bodily signs of adulthood". The body image that they are told is most attractive to men requires them to look younger (and therefore weaker) and more "feminine", where this includes an idea of submission. Hope does not go on to wonder about why men might wish women to appear like this, nor what this wish might represent.

Gross or glamorous?

In 2004 research by sociologists **Merran Toerien** and **Sue Wilkinson** revealed that women's feelings about their body hair had become fairly extreme; women were using words such as "gross", "disgusting"

and "repulsive" to refer to it. By then, full removal of pubic hair had become an item on the beauty agenda in countries from the USA to Australia, even featuring in teen magazines. In their article "Exploring the depilation norm: a qualitative questionnaire study of women's body hair removal" Toerien and Wilkinson note that teen websites were swarming with teenage girls asking if they were "supposed to" shave off their public hair, while popular TV shows such as *Sex and the City* featured discussions about the subject. Advertising and social commentary, said Toerien and Wilkinson, "present it as glamorous, sexy and liberating", but was this how women themselves saw it?

Feminist researchers noted the disappearance of pubic hair from men's adult magazines during the 1990s. In particular, feminists began to look at a section of the media whose audience exploded around the year 2000: internet pornography. The first pornography website was posted in 1994, and by 2010 pornography accounted for 14 per cent of all web searches, according to Dr Ogi Ogas, co-author of *A Billion Wicked Thoughts* (2011). By 2012 the XVideos website alone had 4.4 billion views per month. This was a powerful and widespread cultural messaging medium, and the "money shot" for all porn

> *"If you ask the question, 'Why do 21st-century women feel they have to remove their public hair?' the answer is, 'Because everyone does in porno.'"*
> Caitlin Moran

"Male power is the raison d'être of pornography; the degradation of the female is the means of achieving this power."

Andrea Dworkin

films required that pubic hair did not obscure penetration. There was a practical need on porn sets to "go bare down there".

Feminism and pornography

Liberal and radical feminists had been arguing about the objectification of women within the porn industry for years, and whether porn was expanding or diminishing women's exploration of sexuality, or posing a threat to their autonomy. Liberal feminists such as Drucilla Cornell (b. 1950) tended to reject legal limits on pornography, arguing for freedom of expression. Feminist scholar Carolyn Bronstein notes that radical feminists, on the other hand, analysed the growth in hardcore porn from a more systematic viewpoint, arguing that male-viewed, male-produced, male-profiting hardcore porn was part of a wider, systematic backlash to advances in women's equality. Radicals saw it as one part of an orchestrated campaign to keep women in their assigned social sphere: to "know their place". Radicals such as **Andrea Dworkin** (1946–2005) said that in portraying women as "that thing that causes erection", with an accompanying permission to treat "that thing" as they liked, even with violence, pornography degrades and dehumanizes women in the eyes of all the male viewers (1981).

Is the correlation between internet porn and Brazilian waxing a mere coincidence, or is there a link? Feminist sociologist **Gail Dines** (b. 1958) has researched and written widely on the pornographic industry, and she claims that the vast audience for porn

Key consideration

Why would your partner want you to look like a pre-pubescent girl?

is affecting people's expectations in the real world. The internet has changed everything, she says. In her TED Talk, *Growing Up in a Pornified Culture*, Dines says that "normal" mainstream porn, of the sort that people access on the entry levels of pornographic websites, is routinely violent toward women, both young and old. Given that the average age at which boys start viewing porn is 11, Dines says that this means that porn has become the major form of sex education for children, and they are taking their understanding of "what it is like to be a man" (or woman) from these websites. Online porn is beginning to dictate both boys' and men's ideas about how women should be (and look), as well as the way they can treat women. Internet porn, Dines says, tells men and boys that women are always "up for it" and, in their femininity, "naturally" submissive. They are there for the taking (*see* page 181).

Dines finds that, as a result, boys are becoming desensitized (physically and empathically), limited in their capacity for intimacy and increasingly depressed, while girls and women are finding themselves being expected to act in very particular ways, sexually. Girls surveyed for the Plan International Australia and Our Watch survey (2016) reported feeling under pressure to become a real-life embodiment of what the boys had seen online – to adopt the exaggerated looks, roles and behaviours of porn "stars", and to provide their bodies as though they were merely sex aids. Asked about her first sexual experience, one girl in the survey said, "I think my body looked OK. He seemed to enjoy it." Simone de Beauvoir would have noted the absolute lack of agency, of self as subject, in that short report. The idea that a woman should also gain pleasure from the encounter, was entirely absent.

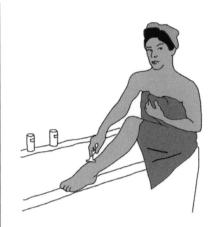

Making a decision:

Dines claims that "this culture is socializing young girls to… hypersexualize and pornify themselves". Part of that is looking like a porn star, which includes "going bare down there". On the flipside, Emma Bailey of trend forecasters WGSN (World's Global Style Network) suggests that women see this as a two-way thing. "As women become more body-confident, eschewing restrictive notions of femininity imposed upon us by a masculine society, the bush is becoming a tool to regain our independence and our voice. A physical manifestation of an increasingly headstrong attitude."

If I get pregnant, can anyone else decide whether I go ahead with it or not?

Monique Wittig • Kate Millett • Annie Besant • Aletta Jacobs • Margaret Sanger •
Diane Munday • Susan Sherwin • Simone de Beauvoir • Judith Jarvis Thomson

In October 2012 a pregnant woman named Savita Halappanavar was admitted to hospital in Ireland suffering from severe pain and miscarrying. Although the pregnancy was not viable, doctors were unable to induce the pregnancy to save her life because there was a foetal heartbeat so an induction would be illegal. Within a few days Savita had miscarried and died of blood poisoning. Her death took place in the 21st century, in a wealthy country, with all the medical equipment needed to save her life on hand. "The law has to change," said her husband. Protesters in countries around the world turned out in their thousands to agree with him, but abortion poses a unique problem for feminism.

In Irish law at the time of Savita's death, the termination of pregnancy (abortion) was illegal, even in "complicated cases" where the pregnancy involved rape, incest, fatal foetal abnormality or a risk to the mother's health. Some countries where it is otherwise illegal do permit abortion in these cases, but the total ban still faces many women around the globe today. In Malta and Haiti, for instance, abortion is illegal under all circumstances, even when the woman's life is at risk. In El Salvador, the possibility of a woman having an abortion is so aggressively policed that women who miscarry or have a stillbirth are routinely suspected of abortion and may be jailed for up to 40 years. Between 1998 and 2013, El Salvador jailed more than 600 women for failed pregnancies.

Essential autonomy

The second-wave feminists of the 1960s (*see* page 13), such as **Monique Wittig** (1935–2003) in France and **Kate Millett** (1934–2017) in the USA, placed the politics of reproduction at the heart of the feminist movement. A woman must have autonomy over her own body, they said. No one should have control of another person's body. This applies in all situations, including pregnancy, when a woman must retain control of decisions about her body – not only in "complicated cases", but all the time. "Free contraception and abortion on demand" was one of the initial four demands by the UK Women's Liberation Movement, agreed at their first national conference in 1970.

In the USA, the Chicago Women's Liberation Union (CWLU) responded to the

Judith Jarvis Thomson proposed this analogy: one night, a Music Society kidnaps you and installs you in a hospital bed. You are the only person with the right blood type to save a dying virtuoso violinist, and they've hooked you up as his life support. If you unplug yourself, he dies. Do you have a moral obligation to stay as an involuntary life support – does the violinist's right to life override your right to decide?

increasing numbers of dangerous "backstreet" abortions by setting up an underground but safe abortion service. Officially called the "Abortion Counseling Service", it was code-named and known to women as "Jane", as documented by author Laura Kaplan in her 1995 book *The Story of Jane*.

These second-wave feminists argued that there are many reasons why a woman may feel unable to retain a pregnancy, including a lack of personal safety (in a relationship or environment), ill heath, lack of financial means (to support a child) or familial support (to be able to work and support a child), or intense psychological problems (particularly when pregnancy occurs as a result of rape).

Industrialization and family size

Feminists who have traced the history of abortion, such as historian Estelle Freedman in her 2002 book *No Turning Back*, have shown that abortion has always been a part of the world. Even in the earliest subsistence cultures, a shortage of food supplies would lead communities to look for ways to limit childbearing, including the use of herbs that might offer contraceptive protection or bring about an abortion. During the agricultural age beginning about 12,000 years ago, children became valuable as workers and so families grew, despite the fact that abortions were easily available and not condemned by religious or secular laws. In North America, all states permitted abortion until

"No woman can call herself free who does not control her own body."
Margaret Sanger

1880, and newspapers were crammed with advertisements for drugs and practitioners offering their services. The only proviso was that the abortion had to be performed before "quickening" – the stage in a pregnancy when a woman could feel the baby move in her womb. This meant that it was up to the mother to determine when life began.

Freedman says that everything changed in 1869, when the Catholic Church – which had until then also recognized quickening as the point of "ensoulment" – outlawed abortion completely. At the same time, industrialization shifted the Western world's thinking about "ideal family size", which dropped from around seven children to four. Men and women wanted fewer children, but abortion had become illegal. The development and distribution of contraceptive devices, through the efforts of **Annie Besant** (1847–1933) in England, **Aletta Jacobs** (1854–1929) in the Netherlands and **Margaret Sanger** (1879–1966) in the USA, gave women new ways in which to control their fertility.

Backlash

As the number of children fell, however, many governments around the world became concerned about the decline in their country's population, and politicians moved to criminalize both contraception and abortion, in the East and West. Communist states, such as the USSR and China, which had offered legal abortions in the 20th century, outlawed them in the 1950s to increase their populations.

> ## Key consideration
> Should anyone other than the woman herself be able to decide what her body must be used for?

Women were encouraged to have more children by a cultural attitude that put mothers on a pedestal, while disparaging the selfish "pleasure seekers" who sought contraception. This was not the full picture, however, as only certain groups of women were encouraged to give birth to more children. Poor women, women of colour and disabled or mentally ill women were not only discouraged, but many were coerced or forced into being sterilized. In the USA, California alone carried out more than 20,000 sterilizations between 1909 and 1979, according to scholars Alexandra Stern and Miroslava Chávez-García. The USA was not alone, and eugenics programmes were adopted in Europe, Latin America, Japan, China and Russia.

A desperate choice

For all these reasons, many women and men are perhaps rightfully suspicious of government motives when the state attempts to interfere in matters of reproduction. From the 1880s to the 1970s, women continued to seek abortions, though these became

> *"At conception and the earliest stage of pregnancy, before quickening, no one believed that a human life existed; not even the Catholic Church took this view."*
> Leslie J Reagan

illegal almost everywhere. The procedures were highly dangerous and caused the deaths of huge numbers of women across the globe. Scholars estimate that by the 1960s a million women were undergoing illegal abortions each year in the USA alone, provided by unskilled backstreet abortionists or by doing it themselves. Veteran women's rights campaigner **Diane Munday** (b. 1931) remembers the horrors involved, and how women's deaths were covered up because of the huge stigma attached to both illegitimate birth and abortion. Each of these options carried huge risks for the pregnant woman.

In areas of the world where illegitimate birth may still result in women being cast out of the home without the means to stay alive, illegal abortions continue to occur in large numbers, according to researchers L B Haddad and N M Nour. In their 2009 paper "Unsafe Abortion: Unnecessary Maternal Mortality" they describe this as a "desperate choice", because each year around 68,000 women worldwide die as a result of unsafe abortions, and five million more will suffer long-term health complications. In Venezuela abortion is the second biggest killer of women aged 12–49, while in India it is estimated that around ten women die of unsafe abortions every day.

It takes two to get pregnant

Feminism differs from other movements or disciplines in its approach to abortion,

feminist philosopher **Susan Sherwin** (b. 1947) points out in her 1991 article "Abortion Through a Feminist Ethics Lens", because feminist analysis focuses on how a woman has become pregnant. She argues that women have a right to autonomy, and for this to be meaningful, it must include the freedom to choose an abortion, because women's subordinate status prevents them from refusing men sexual access to their bodies. The pro-life movement may say that women could just "choose not to have sex", she says, but this oversimplifies the reality. Sexual coercion is a common practice, although some women may not even realize this because they have been socialized into being compliant and accommodating a man's wishes. Women are also subject to rape and reproductive coercion – a type of intimate partner violence in which a male partner forces unprotected sex on the woman in order to get her pregnant against her will. The woman may be aware of this (when it is done using threats) or unaware (where contraception has been tampered with in some form).

Sherwin says that in addition, even though women do not have full control of their sexuality, they are the people held responsible for the care of a child resulting from an unplanned pregnancy. This means that a women is placed in a situation that requires financial stability while also making it impossible for her to work (unless she has

one of the few highly paid jobs available to a woman and can afford childcare). When a women is denied an abortion, and has not acquired a large amount of capital, Sherwin says, she is forced into a relationship of sexual loyalty to the man involved, further perpetuating the cycle of oppression.

Ending the stigma

In the 1970s French women decided to end the stigma attached to abortion and 343 of them published a manifesto in a daily newspaper, testifying that each of them had had abortions. **Simone de Beauvoir** was at the top of the list. Within months, women in Germany had published a similar manifesto, and by the end of the 1970s, France, West Germany, Italy, India and the UK had liberalized their abortion laws. In 1973 the famous court case of Roe v Wade took place in the USA, with the court ruling that the state could not interfere with a woman's right to choose abortion during the first six months of pregnancy. Within a year of this ruling, the death rates of women from abortion had fallen from 18 to 3 per 100,000 women in the USA.

Making a decision:

Intersectional feminists have begun to focus on the idea of "reproductive justice", rather than "freedom to choose", pointing out that if society supported mothers and children more – helping pregnant women and mothers stay in work or education, access healthcare and be sure of a safe home – the cultural change would inevitably lead to fewer abortions. Radical and socialist feminists may applaud this aim, but say that while this is not the case, women should not be left with only a "desperate choice". They point also to the moral argument made by American philosopher **Judith Jarvis Thomson** (b. 1929): that if women have rights over their own bodies, then they also have the right not to have their bodies used by others against their will. Which means that wherever those rights are politically and legally enshrined, you alone have the freedom to decide what to do if you discover that you are pregnant.

Why am I afraid to walk down the street?

Sylvia Walby • Catharine MacKinnon • Kate Millett • Adrienne Rich
• Andrea Dworkin • Susan Brownmiller

The feminist view of violence against women, by people known to them or by strangers, differs from its portrayal in mainstream media. As **Sylvia Walby** (b. 1953) notes in her 1990 book *Theorizing Patriarchy*, "the conventional view...holds that rape and battering are isolated instances caused by psychological problems in a few men". Walby goes on to explain that within feminism, however, "male violence against women is considered to be part of a system of controlling women". This system is patriarchy, and feminists maintain that the threat of violence is its strongest tool for keeping the system in place.

Walby drew attention to the many different forms of feminism, and offered a unifying analysis. She said that patriarchy operates in six forms: in the home (where women are expected to work for free, conforming to the expectations of their male partners); in the working world (where women will be met with discriminatory pay, practices and treatment); in the state (where laws are fundamentally biased toward men): through patriarchal institutions (including religion, education and the media, which position women through a patriarchal viewpoint); patriarchal sexual relations (where the genders are viewed as complying to different social norms and expectations); and male violence. This last item, Walby says, is not random or attributable to the intentions of individual men. It operates under patterned and systemic criteria.

Walby looks at the work of radicals such as **Catharine MacKinnon** (b. 1946), **Kate**

Millett (1934–2017) and **Adrienne Rich** (1929–2012), who suggest that men sexually objectify women, reducing them to "mere sex objects".

This objectification, they say, stretches beyond the conventionally sexual arenas into

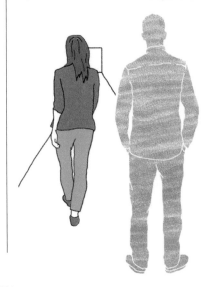

> *"Funny, every man I meet wants to protect*
> *me. I can't figure out what from."*
> Mae West

all areas of life – including the workplace – and is experienced by women in the various forms of sexual harassment. The role of heterosexuality within patriarchy is to establish a power dynamic between male and female; Walby describes it as a "central institution in men's domination over women". This means that sexuality and power dynamics are intrinsically linked. **Andrea Dworkin** (1946–2005) explored this link through the investigation of heterosexual pornography, Walby notes, and found that it commonly contained the "violent sexual domination and humiliation of the women involved". If men simultaneously sexualize women and dominate them, Walby argues, "sexuality is the terrain or medium through which men dominate women".

Part of the social structure

Male violence against women – including rape, sexual assault, intimate-partner violence, sexual harassment and child sexual abuse – can only be understood as an essential part of a patriarchal social structure, according to Walby. These actions lie on a continuum, with wolf-whistles at one end and rape/child sexual abuse at the other, she says. But what leads some men to attack women while others don't? Walby looked at the liberal analysis of rape, which contends that it is carried out by men with severe psychological problems who have failed "to acquire the normal form of masculinity"

due to childhood problems. But if this were so, Walby argues, most rapists would be referred to psychiatrists during or after court proceedings, but this happens only very rarely; it is not recognized as an extreme psychological phenomenon. Also, this theory would seem to predict very few rapes, whereas the figures in every society are extremely high (this is backed up by global estimates published by the World Health Organization, or WHO, in 2016, indicating that around 35 per cent of women worldwide have experienced physical and/or sexual male violence).

Theorists have also suggested that class holds the answer, Walby notes. The idea here is that men at the bottom of the class hierarchy are violent toward women because of the frustration generated by their circumstances. When under extreme economic stress, they lash out at their female partners. This theory developed further to suggest that a deviant sub-culture of violence developed at the bottom of the social order, where working-class men developed different values from other men as a result of their alienation from the system. But both of these arguments for class as a reason for rape would result in a disproportionate number of working-class men being rapists, which is not borne out by the evidence. A huge study by Diana Russell (b. 1938), "The prevalence and incidence of forcible rape and attempted rape of females" (1982), Walby notes, shows an equal distribution of rapists across all classes. The same study showed that there was not an unequal distribution according to race, either, as has also been suggested. The ethnicity of rapists has been shown to reflect the same proportion of its representation in the population. And neither the argument from class or race can explain why these men are taking out their "frustrations" on women, rather than the general, mixed population. Any credible theory for why men sexually attack women, Walby said, must take into account the essential elements of gender and sexuality.

The normalization of rape

In 1975 the radical feminist **Susan Brownmiller** (b. 1935) published *Against Our Will*, a huge study of the history of rape. She found that forcible seizure and rape of a woman was so common among the Ancient Babylonians and other cultures that a "bride price" was established; this was to be paid to the girl's, or woman's, father in recompense for having devalued her price as a bride. Her value was codified in Babylonian, Mosaic and Greek law as 50 pieces of silver. This is how rape entered the law, Brownmiller records, as a crime against a father – "an embezzlement of his daughter's fair price on the market".

> ## Key consideration
>
> Why are men's ideas of what women want given priority over what women actually want?

Rape also became a common act for victors triumphant in war (which continues today), because it is used to illustrate the total defeat of a population (the vanquished men are too powerless even to protect "their" women) and it introduces the conqueror's offspring into the defeated men's bloodline. Men see rape as the act of a conqueror, Brownmiller suggests. It makes them feel triumphant.

Brownmiller also traces the history of responsibility for rape, as it moved from resting solely on the men toward somehow involving the women. In Ancient Hebrew culture, for instance, a married woman who was raped was stoned to death along with her attacker. The reasoning given by the elders was that "if the girl had screamed she would have been rescued". Brownmiller notes that

> *"His forcible entry into her body, despite her physical protestations and struggle, became the vehicle of his victorious conquest over her being, the ultimate test of his superior strength, the triumph of his manhood."*
> Susan Brownmiller

> *"My takeaway was that rape was a deliberate act of power, dominance, and humiliation committed by men with no moral compass — and that most victims feared their attackers were going to kill them."*
> Susan Brownmiller

some of the faulty reasoning used thousands of years ago, such as this, can still be heard in courtrooms across the world today.

There are "four deadly myths", she says, that men fall back on to defend themselves against the crime of rape. First, "all women want to be raped". This idea does away with the idea of consent, suggesting that even when women say "no" they really mean "yes". It is important to men to believe this, Brownmiller suggests, because if rape is done in the name of masculinity, then it is convenient to say that femininity is in agreement. This allows rapists to tell themselves that they have done nothing wrong, and it often crops up in popular culture, such as in Robin Thicke's 2013 song "Blurred Lines", "Baby, it's in your nature... I know you want it".

The second myth is that "no woman can be raped against her will". This idea backs up the first, suggesting that all women "do really want to be raped". In courts, lawyers have "made jokes" about the inability to thread a moving needle, Brownmiller says. In legal terms, it led to the idea of "forcible rape" (leaving the nonsensical idea of non-forcible rape, which journalist Erika Eichelberger later noted was still in use in 2011, when US Republicans used this idea to limit funded abortions to "forcible" rapes only).

Third is the myth, "she was asking for it". Brownmiller says this is "the classic way a

rapist shifts the burden from himself to the victim". It says that something about the woman was enough to precipitate rape (such as her short skirt, her "incautious behaviour", her sexual past). In no other crime is this suggested of the victim, Brownmiller says. If someone is murdered, no one wonders whether it was his or her fault – whether they "precipitated" it. The crime has been committed. The tragedy of this myth, she says, is that the insecurity of women runs so deep that many, possibly most, rape victims agonize afterward about what it was "in their behaviour, their manner, their dress, that triggered this awful act against them". When, in fact, it is nothing more than "a part of the smokescreen that men throw up to obscure their actions".

Fourth is the myth that "if you're going to be raped, you might as well relax and

enjoy it". This is employed to deliberately make light of the physical violation of rape. It also tells women that they must accept two things: first, that male triumph is inevitable, and second, whatever you think really, "all women want to be raped". Even when women have tried to save themselves by pretending to buy into this myth, Brownmiller notes – such as those killed by the Boston Strangler, who tried to cooperate and "just get it over with" – they were still murdered.

None of these myths are remotely true, says Brownmiller. And the last line of defence – that "women cry rape with ease and glee" – bears no relation to reality, she says. The reality is that victimized women have always been reluctant to report rape, because of the shame of public exposure, the double standard that makes them feel somehow culpable for any act of sexual aggression committed against them, and the fear of possible retribution from the assailant. And also because they have "come to the realistic conclusion that their accounts are received with a harsh cynicism" that means they will not be believed.

Making a decision:

You are afraid to walk down a dark street alone, says Brownmiller, because "the ultimate effect of rape upon the woman's mental and emotional health has been accomplished *even without the act*". The knowledge that there is always the possibility of rape is enough. The threat is useful to patriarchy, she says, because if women "accept a special burden of self-protection", it will reinforce the idea that they "must live and move about in fear – and can never expect to achieve the personal freedom, independence and self-assurance of men". It keeps women in the birdcage, as Marilyn Frye suggested (*see* page 24), even though the door is open.

Bibliography

Key feminist sources referred to throughout:

De Beauvoir, Simone (1949, 1953 English edition) *The Second Sex.* London: Jonathan Cape.

Code, Lorraine (ed) (2004 [2000]) *The Encyclopedia of Feminist Theories.* London and New York: Routledge

Firestone, Shulamith (1970) *The Dialectic of Sex: The Case For Feminist Revolution.* William & Morrow Company.

Freedman, Estelle B. (2002) *No Turning Back: the history of feminism and the future of women.* New York: Ballantine Books.

Friedan, Betty (2010 [1963]) *The Feminine Mystique.* London: Penguin Classics

Greer, Germaine (2012 [1970]) *The Female Eunuch.* London: Fourth Estate/Harper Collins

hooks, bell (2000) *All About Love* New York: Harper Perennial

Lorde, Audre (2017) *Your Silence Will Not Protect You.* London: Silver Press.

Millett, Kate and Mackinnon, Catharine (1983 [1970]) *Sexual Politics.* New York: Colombia University Press

Rowbotham, Sheila (2015 [1973]) *Women's Consciousness, Man's World.* London: Verso.

Steinem, Gloria (1995 [1983]) *Outrageous Acts And Everyday Rebellions,* 2nd ed. USA: Henry Holt and Company

Wolf, Naomi (1991) *The Beauty Myth.* London: Vintage/Random House

Wollstonecraft, Mary. (1792) *A Vindication of the Rights of Woman.* London: J. Johnson.

List of other sources quoted from/alluded to:

Chapter 1: Politics & Power
What is a feminist?

Adichie, Chimamanda Ngozi. (2015) *We Should All Be Feminists.* New York: Anchor Books.

Aristotle (2008 [350 BCE]), trans. Benjamin Jowett *Politics* (Book One). New York: Cosimo Classics

Freedman, Estelle B. (Eds.) (2007) *The essential feminist reader.* New York: Modern Library.

Hanisch, Carol. (1970) "The Personal Is Political" in *Notes from the Second Year: Women's Liberation* (eds. Shulamith Firestone and Anne Koedt). New York: Radical Feminism.

Spender, Dale. (1985) *Man Made Language.* London: Routledge & Kegan Paul.

Truth, Sojourner. (1851). "Ain't I a Woman?". *Civil Rights and Conflict in the United States: Selected Speeches.* Lit2Go Edition.

I've already got the same rights as men, haven't I?

Amnesty International (2015) "Shamed and Blamed: Pregnant girls' Rights at Risk in Sierra Leone", London: Amnesty International Publications

Neuwirth, Jessica (2005) "Inequality Before the Law: Holding States Accountable for Sex Discriminatory Laws Under the Convention on the Elimination of All Forms of Discrimination Against Women and Through the Beijing Platform for Action", *Harvard Human Rights Journal,* 18, pp19–54

Solnit, Rebecca (2014) *Men Explain Things to Me.* Chicago and New York: Haymarket Books

United Nations Children's Fund (2014) "Ending Child Marriage: Progress and prospects", New York: UNICEF

United Nations Women (2011) *Progress of the World's Women: In Pursuit of Justice.* New York, United Nations Publications

Why should I bother to vote? It won't affect my personal life.

Amos, Howard. "Pussy Riot's Mariya Alyokhina: 'Politics is not something that exists in one or another White House. It is our lives'" *The Guardian,* 1 September 2017

Why do unknown men call me "sweetheart" and "honey"?

Brown, Roger & Gilman, Albert (1960) "The Pronouns of Power and Solidarity", in Sebeok, T A (ed) (1960) *Style in Language,* pp253–76, New York and London: MIT and John Wiley & Sons

Frye, Marilyn (1983). "The Systemic Birdcage of Sexism" in *The Politics of Reality: essays in feminist theory.* California: Crossing Press.

What's wrong with saying that women are more compassionate than men?

Jackman, Mary. (1994). *The Velvet Glove: Paternalism and conflict in gender, class and race relations.* Berkeley, CA: University of California Press.

Glick, Peter & Fiske, Susan T. (1996) "The Ambivalent Sexism Inventory: Differentiating Hostile and Benevolent Sexism". March 1996, *Journal of Personality and Social Psychology* 70(3):491–512

Glick, Peter & Fiske, Susan T. (1997) "Hostile and Benevolent Sexism: Measuring Ambivalent Sexist Attitudes Toward Women". *Psychology of Women Quarterly* 1997 21: 119

Gokova, Johah (1998) "Challenging Men to Reject Gender Stereotypes". *Sexual Health Exchange.* 1998;(2):1-3.

Lee, T. L., Fiske, S. T., Glick, P., & Chen, Z. (2010). "Ambivalent Sexism in Close Relationships: (Hostile) Power and (Benevolent) Romance Shape Relationship Ideals." *Sex Roles,* 62:7-8, pp583–601. http://doi.org/10.1007/s11199-010-9770-x

Is feminism just a white woman's thing?

Aptheker, Bettina. (1989). *Tapestries of life: women's work, women's consciousness, and the meaning of daily experience.* Amherst: University of Massachusetts Press.

Combahee River Collective (1977/2016). "A Black Feminist Statement". In: S. Mann & A. Patterson, ed., *Reading Feminist Theory: From Modernity to Postmodernity.* Oxford: OUP, pp.247–252.

Crenshaw, Kimberlé (1989) "Demarginalizing the Intersection of Race and Sex". *University of Chicago Legal Forum,* Vol. 1989, Issue 1, Article 8.

hooks, bell. 1981. *Ain't I a Woman : Black Women and Feminism,* Boston: South End Press.

Rich, Adrienne. (1985) "Notes Towards a Politics of Location", in Diaz-Diocaretz, M. & Zavala, I. (eds) *Women, Feminist Identity and Society in the 1980s: Selected Papers.* Amsterdam: John Benjamin.

Yuval-Davis, Nira, (1994). "Women, Ethnicity and Empowerment. Shifting Identities Shifting Racisms". Special issue of *Feminism and Psychology* 14 (1): pp179–98.

Why doesn't feminism ever get us equality?

Faludi, Susan. (2006). *Backlash: the undeclared war against American women.* New York: Crown Publishing Group: Three Rivers Press

Ipsos Mori Survey (2017). Global Views on Women's Equality.

Monroe, Julie A. "A Feminist Vindication of Mary Wollstonecraft." *Iowa Journal of Literary Studies* 8 (1987): pp143–152.

Santee, Barbara. "Letter to a Young Activist: Do Not Drop the Banner". *On the Issues Magazine,* Fall 2012.

Woolf, Virginia (1932/1988). *The Essays of Virginia Woolf,* Volume III. Chatto & Windus.

Chapter 2: Dating & Relationships
The man I'm dating insists on paying for everything? Should I let him?

Belk, R and Coon, G (1991) "Can't Buy Me Love: Dating, Money and Gifts." *Advances in Consumer Research* Volume 18, 1991

Korman, S and Leslie, G (1982) "The relationship of feminist ideology and date expense sharing to perceptions of sexual aggression in dating," *The Journal of Sex Research.* 18:2, pp.114–129.

Match.com (2017) Singles In America Survey http://www.singlesinamerica.com/2017/

Bibliography

Steinem, Gloria (1993) *Revolution From Within: A Book of Self Esteem.* Little, Brown US

Can I use online dating apps without objectifying myself?

OkCupid (2009) How Your Race Affects The Messages You Get. [https://theblog.okcupid.com/how-your-race-affects-the-messages-you-get-39c68771b99e]

YouGov (2017) Naked Photo Survey. [https://today.yougov.com/news/2017/10/09/53-millennial-women-have-received-dick-pic/]

What's wrong with one-night stands?

Ehrman, M (1994) "Susie Bright Tells All : Preaching a Doctrine of Adventure, Fantasy and Safety, the Feminist Bad Girl Brings Her Pro-Sex Message to the Masses." *LA Times.*

Vance, Carole S. (1984) *Pleasure and Danger: Toward a Politics of Sexuality.* Boston: Routledge & Kegan Paul

Why can't I tell my partner I am faking it?

Durex, (2017) The Orgasm Gap. [https://www.durex.co.uk/en-gb/explore-sex/article/the-orgasm-gap]

Koedt, Anne (1970) *The Myth of the Vaginal Orgasm.* Somerville: New England Press

Masters, W and Johnson, V (1966) *Human Sexual Response.* New York: Ishi Press International

Reiner, R. (1989) *When Harry Met Sally.* Castle Rock Entertainment, Nelson Entertainment. USA: Colombia Pictures.

Stoltenberg, John (1999 [1989]) *Refusing To Be A Man: Essays on Social Justice: Essays on Sex and Justice.* Oxford: Routledge

I'm happy and successful. Who cares if I have a partner?

Steinem, G (1993) *Revolution From Within: A Book of Self Esteem.* Little, Brown US

Can my boyfriend be a feminist?

Fitzpatrick, M. K., Salgado, D. M., Suvak, M. K., King, L. A., & King, D. W. (2004). Associations of Gender and Gender-Role Ideology With Behavioral and Attitudinal Features of Intimate Partner Aggression. *Psychology of Men & Masculinity.*

hooks, bell (2000) *Feminism is for Everybody: Passionate Politics.* London: Pluto Press

Jardine, A. and Smith, P (eds) (1987) *Men in Feminism.* New York and London: Routledge.

Jensen, R (2017) *The End of The Patriarchy: Radical Feminism for Men.* Melbourne: Spinifex Press

Mill, John Stuart (1869) *The Subjection of Women.* London: Green, Reader And Dyer.

Rudman, L and Phelan, J (2007) *The Interpersonal Power of Feminism: Is Feminism Good for Romantic Relationships?* Springer Science & Business Media

Truman, D, Tokar, D, Fischer, A (1996) "Dimensions of masculinity: Relations to date rape supportive attitudes and sexual aggression in dating situations." *Journal of Counseling and Development -* Volume 74.

Walters, M (2005) *Feminism: A Very Short Introduction.* Oxford: OUP

I want to propose to my boyfriend. Can I?

The AP-WE tv Poll (2014) Conducted by GfK Public Affairs & Corporate Communications. http://surveys.ap.org/data/GfK/AP-WEtv%20January%202014%20Poll%20POSTED%20Final_VALENTINES.pdf

Butler, Judith (2007 [1990]) *Gender Trouble.* Oxford: Routledge

Sassler, S and Miller, A J (2011) "Waiting To Be Asked: Gender, Power, and Relationship Progression Among Cohabiting Couples." *Journal of Family Issues.*

Chapter 3: Marriage & Domestic Life

Fairy-tale wedding, fairy-tale marriage?

Calhoun, A, (2017) *Wedding Toasts I'll Never Give.* WW Norton & Co.

Friedman, M (2003) *Autonomy, Gender, Politics.* Oxford: OUP

Gay, R (2014) *Bad Feminist.* New York: Harper Collins

Greer, Germaine (2004) "The Middle-Class Myth of Love and Marriage" in *Feminisms and Womanisms,* (eds. Althea Price and Susan Silva-Wayne), Toronto: Women's Press

James, E.L (2012) *Fifty Shades of Grey,* London: Cornerstone

The Knot (2016) The National Cost of a Wedding Hits $35,329 [https://www.theknot.com/content/average-wedding-cost-2016]

Should I taking my partner's name after marriage?

Langer, E (2017) Kate Millett, 'high priestess' of second-wave feminism, dies at 82. The Washington Post [https://www.washingtonpost.com/local/obituaries/kate-millett-high-priestess-of-second-wave-feminism-dies-at-82/2017/09/07/1ccfa2b6-93d4-11e7-aace-04b862b2b3f3_story.html?utm_term=.d17eb642a33b]

YouGov Survey (2016) [https://yougov.co.uk/news/2016/09/13/six-ten-women-would-like-take-their-spouses-/]

My husband and I both work. Why do I do all the housework?

Johnston, Jill (1973) *Lesbian Nation: The Feminist Solution.* Touchstone

Kornrich, S, Brines, J, Leupp K (2013) "Egalitariansim, Housework, and Sexual Frequency in Marriage." *American Sociology Review* [https://www.ncbi.nlm.nih.gov/pmc/articles/PMC4273893/#R73]

Brady, Judy, *I Want A Wife, Literature for Composition,* (Third Edition) HarperCollins Customs Books

Hochschild, Airlie R. (2012 [1989]) *The Second Shift.* Penguin Books.

Do I even want kids?

The Economist 2017) The Rise of childlessness [https://www.economist.com/news/international/21725553-more-adults-are-not-having-children-much-less-worrying-it-appears-rise]

Moran, Caitlin (2012) *How To Be A Woman.* London: Ebury Press

Rich, Adrienne. (1977). *Of Woman Born.* London: Virago.

What is a normal family anyway?

Millett, Kate (2000) *Flying.* University of Illinois Press

Who should take parental leave?

Haas L and Hwang C, "The Impact of Taking Parental Leave on Fathers' Participation In Childcare And Relationships With Children: Lessons from Sweden" http://www.tandfonline.com/doi/abs/10.1080/13668800701785346

Noland, M, Moran, T, Kotschwar, B (2016) Is Gender Diversity Profitable? Evidence From a Global Survey [https://piie.com/publications/wp/wp16-3.pdf]

Reeves, R and Sawhill, I (2015) Men's Lib! *The New York Times* [https://www.nytimes.com/2015/11/15/opinion/sunday/mens-lib.html]

My daughter insists on being called princess.

Criado-Perez, C (2015) *Do It Like A Woman:... And Change The World.* London: Portobello Books

Fine, Cordelia (2010) *Delusions of Gender: How Our Minds, Society, and Neurosexism Create Difference.* London: Icon Books

The BBC Stories, Girls Toys vs Boys Toys: The Experiment, [https://www.youtube.com/watch?v=nWu44AqF0iI] [https://www.theiet.org/index.cfm] [https://www.ons.gov.uk/employmentandlabourmarket/peopleinwork/employmentandemployeetypes/datasets/employmentbyoccupationemp04]

Chapter 4: Work & Pay

I just want to be a homemaker. Is that OK?

Albert, P. R. (2015). Why is depression more prevalent in women? *Journal of Psychiatry & Neuroscience :* JPN, 40(4), 219–221. http://doi.org/10.1503/jpn.150205

Brontë , Charlotte (1847). *Jane Eyre.* London: Smith, Elder & Co.

Evans, Stephen. 14 February 2016. "The world's best bakers - and they aren't French". BBC News (Accessed online, 28 December 2017, at

Bibliography

Gilbert, Sandra M., & Gubar, Susan (2000; 18th edition). *The Madwoman in the Attic*. New Haven, Yale University Press.

Mitchell, Silas Weir (1878) *Fat and Blood*. 2nd Edition. Philadelphia: J.B. Lippincott and Co.

Showalter, Elaine. (1985). *The Female Malady: Women, madness and English culture 1830–1980*. London: Virago.

Woolf, Virginia (1931) "Professions for Women." Speech, 21 Jan. 1931, National Society for Women's Service.

Why am I working for less pay than him?

Babcock, L., & Laschever, S. (2003). *Women don't ask: Negotiation and the gender divide*. Princeton, N.J: Princeton University Press.

Ferguson, Ann (1991) *Sexual Democracy: Women, Oppression and Revolution*. Boulder Colorado: Westview Press.

Hoff Summers, Christina: "Wage Gap Myth Exposed – By Feminists" Huffpost Blog, 11 April 2012, [https://www.huffingtonpost.com/christina-hoff-sommers/wage-gap_b_2073804.html]

Sandberg, S., & Scovell, N. (2013). *Lean in: Women, work, and the will to lead*. New York: Penguin Random House

Saul, J. M. (2003). *Feminism: Issues & arguments*. Oxford: OUP.

Walby, Sylvia. (1990). *Theorizing patriarchy*. Oxford, UK: B. Blackwell.

Women in Computing articles: [https://hackernoon.com/a-brief-history-of-women-in-computing-e7253ac24306]

[https://www.npr.org/sections/alltechconsidered/2014/10/06/345799830/the-forgotten-female-programmers-who-created-modern-tech

[https://www.smithsonianmag.com/smart-news/computer-programming-used-to-be-womens-work-718061/]

World Economic Forum, The Global Gender Gap Report 2017 [http://www3.weforum.org/docs/WEF_GGGR_2017.pdf]

Am I too nice to be the boss?

Catalyst. (2007). "The double-bind dilemma for women in leadership: Damned if you do, doomed if you don't." New York.

Clinton, Hillary (2009) [https://www.popsugar.com/love/Hillary-Clinton-December-2009-Vogue-Interview-6278290]

Connolly, Kate. (2005) "Let's follow the path Thatcher pioneered, says Germany's Iron Maiden." The Telegraph, 15 July 2005 (accessed online 2 January 2017, http://www.telegraph.co.uk/news/worldnews/europe/germany/1494103/Lets-follow-the-path-Thatcher-pioneered-says-Germanys-Iron-Maiden.html)

Eagly, Alice H. (2007) "Female leadership advantage and disadvantage". *Psychology of Women Quarterly*, 31, pp.1–12.

Gallup's annual Work & Education poll, August 7_11, 2013 http://news.gallup.com/poll/165791/americans-prefer-male-boss.aspx

Glick, P and Fiske, S. (2007). "Sex discrimination: the psychological approach". In F. Crosby (Ed.), *Sex discrimination in the workplace*. Malen, MA: Blackwell.

Kanter, Rosabeth Moss. (1993) *Men and Women of the Corporation*. 2nd edn. New York: HarperCollins

When I was renegotiating my salary my boss said he was "aware that he might be dazzling me with percentages".

Chesler, Phyllis (2005). *Women and Madness*. New York, NY: Palgrave Macmillan.

Cresswell, R., & Schneider, J. G. (1862). *Aristotle's History of animals: In ten books*. London: H.G. Bohn.

Moreton, C. (2013) "Why Boys are Better at Exams". *The Daily Telegraph*, 18 August 2013.

Rousseau, Jean-Jacques (1923 [1762]), *The Social Contract*; trans. G D H Cole, London: J M Dent & Sons

Wardle, Martin (1951). *Mary Wollstonecraft: A Critical Biography*. University of Kansas Press

My boss is insisting I wear high heels to work. Is this legal?

Bilefsky, Dan,. "Sent Home for Not Wearing Heels, She Ignited a British Rebellion". *The New York Times*, 25 January 2017

House of Commons, 291. (25 January 2017.) "High heels and workplace dress codes: first join report of session 2016–17". HOC London.

Marie Claire (25 August 2016) "#BurkiniBan: This is what happens when police tell women what to wear on the beach."

Rubin, Alissa J. (27 August 2016) "From Bikinis to Burkinis, Regulating What Women Wear". *The New York Times*

Topham, Gwyn. (5 February 2016) "Female British Airways cabin crew win the right to wear trousers'. *The Guardian*.

Must I go drinking with male colleagues to get ahead?

Berdahl, Jennifer F. (2007) "Harassment Based on Sex: Protecting Social Status in the Context of Gender Hierarchy". *The Academy of Management Review*, April 2007, vol 32:2

Maass, Anne; Cadinu Mara; Guarnieri, Gaia; Grasselli, Annalisa. "Sexual Harassment Under Social Identity Threat: The Computer Harassment Paradigm". *Journal of Personality & Social Psychology*. 2003;85:853–870.

Macmillian, Ross, and Gartner, Rosemary. (1999) "When She Brings Home the Bacon: Labor-Force Participation and the Risk of Spousal Violence against Women. *Journal of Marriage & the Family* 61: 947-958

Mathis, W., Dobner, J. and Stevens, T. "Some Utahns say men and women should keep their distance at the office and beyond. That may be holding women back." *Salt Lake Tribune*, 13 August 2017.

McLaughlin, H., Uggen, C., & Blackstone, A. (2012). "Sexual Harassment, Workplace Authority, and the Paradox of Power". *American Sociological Review*, 77(4), 625–647. http://doi.org/10.1177/0003122412451728

Quinn, Beth, A. (2002) "Sexual Harassment & Masculinity: The Power & Meaning of 'Girl Watching'." *Gender & Society*, V16:3, 386-402

Strauss, Eric M., "Iowa Woman Fired for Being Attractive Looks Back and Moves On" ABC News: 2 August, 2013

Valenti, Jessica. (31 March 2017) "Mike Pence doesn't eat alone with women. That speaks volumes." *The Guardian*.

Willer, R., Rogalin, C., Conlon, B. & Wojnowicz, M. (2013) "Overdoing Gender: A test of the masculine overcompensation thesis"

Do women have to be naked to get into the Met. Museum?

Bollen, C. (15 February 2012) "Guerrilla Girls" *Interview Magazine*.

English Heritage (29 February 2016) "Why were Women Written out of History? An interview with Bettany Hughes". http://blog.english-heritage.org.uk/women-written-history-interview-bettany-hughes/

Nochlin, Linda (1988). "Why Have There Been No Great Woman Artists?" *Women, Art & Power & Other Essays*, Boulder: Westview Press

The Times (11/3/1914). "National Gallery Outrage: Suffragist Prisoner in Court." http://www.heretical.com/suffrage/1914tms2.html

Watson, James D. (2011) *The Double Helix: A Personal Account of the Discovery of the Structure of DNA*. New York: Simon & Schuster

Chapter 5: Women in the Media

Dare I share my opinions online?

Amnesty International (2017) Black & Asian women MPs abused more online [https://www.amnesty.org.uk/online-violence-women-mps]

Klein, K and Hawthorne, S (ed.) (1999) *CyberFeminism: Connectivity, Critique and Creativity: Fletcher, B 'Cyberfiction: A Fictional Journey Into Cyberspace (or How I became a Cyberfeminist)*. Melbourne: Spinifex Press

Moss, Tara (2017) "Cyberhate and Beyond: Tara Moss at The National Press Club'"

Penny, Laurie (2013) *Cybersexism: Sex, Gender and Power On The Internet*. London: Bloomsbury Publishing.

Symantec, (2016) 'Norton Study Shows Online Harassment Nears Epidemic Proportions for Young Australian Women' [https://www.symantec.com/en/au/about/newsroom/press-releases/2016/symantec_0309_01]

Why am I obsessed with what female celebrities look like?

Bibliography

Berger, John (2008) *Ways of Seeing*. Penguin Modern Classics.

Lawrence, J (2017) *The Hollywood Reporter* Awards Chatter Podcast [https://www.hollywoodreporter.com/race/awards-chatter-podcast-jennifer-lawrence-mother-1059777]

Paglia, Camille (2015) "Can group selfies advance women's goals?" *The Hollywood Reporter*

Sontag, Susan (1979) *On Photography*. London: Penguin Books

Walters, M (2005) *Feminism: A Very Short Introduction*. Oxford: OUP.

Maybe I'm not as straight as I thought…

Butler, Judith (2007 [1990]) *Gender Trouble*. Oxford: Routledge

Johnston, Jill (1973) *Lesbian Nation: The Feminist Solution*. Touchstone

Onlywomen Press Collective (1981) *Love Your Enemy? The Debate Between Heterosexual Feminism and Political Lesbianism*

Rieger, G, Department of Psychology at the University of Essex [http://www.telegraph.co.uk/women/sex/10624669/Lesbian-sex-life-Avoid-measuring-your-sex-life-by-how-often-you-do-it.html]

University of Waterloo (2018) 'Digital Technology is Helping Women Explore Their Sexuality' (*The Journal of Sexuality and Culture*)

Why can't I stop buying new clothes?

Harvard Business Review (2009) *The Female Economy* [https://hbr.org/2009/09/the-female-economy]

hooks, b (1992) "Eating the Other: Desire and Resistance." Boston: South End Spice.

Where are all the women in film?

"IBM is using bollywood movies to identify and neutralize gender bias" [https://qz.com/1102088/ibm-is-using-bollywood-movies-to-identify-and-neutralize-gender-bias/]

Bigelow, K (2009) *The Hurt Locker*

Gay, Roxane (2014) *Bad Feminist*. New York: Harper Collins

Mulvey, Laura (1975) 'Visual Pleasure and Narrative Cinema', *Screen*

See Jane, [https://seejane.org/gender-in-media-news-release/new-study-geena-davis-institute-finds-archery-catches-fire-thanks-inspiring-hollywood-images/]

Woolf, Virginia (2002 [1928]) *A Room of One's Own*, Penguin

Why do we need women's magazines?

Smith, Barbara "A Press of our Own: Kitchen Table: Women of Color Press" [https://www.jstor.org/stable/3346433?seq=1#page_scan_tab_contents]

Women's Media Centre (2017) Divided 2017: The Media Gender Gap [http://www.womensmediacenter.com/reports/divided-2017]

Woolf, Virginia (2002 [1928]) *A Room of One's Own*, Penguin

Is technology sexist?

Haraway, Donna 1985 "A Cyborg Manifesto: Science, Technology, and Socialist-Feminism in the Late Twentieth Century", *The Berkeley Socialist Review Collective*

Penny, Laurie (2013) *Cybersexism: Sex, Gender and Power On The Internet*. London: Bloomsbury Publishing.

Penny, Laurie (2016) "Why do we give robots female names? Because we don't want to consider their feelings" London: *The New Statesman*

Treneman, A, *The Independent*.

http://www.independent.co.uk/life-style/interview-sadie-plant-it-girl-for-the-21st-century-1235380.html

WEC (2016) The Industry Gender Gap: Women and Work In The Fourth Industrial Revolution. http://www3.weforum.org/docs/WEF_FOJ_Executive_Summary_GenderGap.pdf

Weingberger, D *The LA Review of Books* [http://https/lareviewofbooks.org/article/rethinking-knowledge-internet-age/]

Chapter 6: It's My Body

Why do I always feel fat?

Clements, Kirstie (2013) *The Vogue Factor*. London: Guardian Faber

Edwards, Emily (2007) 'Are Eating Disorders Feminist?, Power,

Resistance, & the Feminine Ideal'. *Perspectives on Power Quest conference*

Marketdata (2017) *The U.S. Weight Loss & Diet Control Market* (14th edition). Marketdata Enterprises Inc., Florida.

Orbach, Susie. (1978). *Fat is a feminist issue*. New York: Paddington Press.

Willliams, Zoe. (2016) "Susie Orbach: 'Not all women used to have eating issues. Now everybody does". *The Guardian*

If men could have babies, would everything change?

Boden Alison. L. (2007) "Theological Challenges to Religious Women's Rights." *Women's Rights and Religious Practice*. London: Palgrave Macmillan,

Delaney, J.; Lupton M. J., (1976) *The Curse: A Cultural History of Menstruation*. New York: Dutton

Lerner, Gera. (1986) *The Creation of Patriarchy*. New York: OUP.

Pope John Paul II (1995), "Letter to Women" http://www.ewtn.com/library/PAPALDOC/JP2WOM.htm

Van Nieuwkerk, Karin (1988) "An hour for God and an hour for the heart: Islam, gender and female entertainment in Egypt." in *Egypt, Music and Anthropology* 3.

Do I really need to go bare down there?

Bronstein, C. (2011) *Battling Pornography: The American Feminist Anti-Pornography Movement, 1976–1986*. Cambridge: Cambridge University Press.

Cornell, D.,(ed.) (2000), *Feminism and Pornography*, Oxford: OUP

Dines, G. (2010). *Pornland: How porn has hijacked our sexuality*. Boston: Beacon Press.

Dines, Gail (2016) Ted Talk: *Pornified Culture*. Retrieved from: https://www.youtube.com/watch?v=_YpHNImNsx8

Dworkin, Andrea (1981). *Pornography: Men possessing women*. London: Women's Press.

Hope, Christine (1982) "Caucasian Female Body Hair and American Culture" *The Journal of American Culture*, Vol 5:1.

Ogas, O., & Gaddam, S. (2011). *A billion wicked thoughts*. New York: Dutton/Penguin Books.

Plan International Australia (2016) "Don't send me that pic." Melbourne, Australia: Plan International Australia and Our Watch.

Toerien, M and Wilkinson, S (2004) "Exploring the depilation norm: A qualitative questionnaire study of women's body hair removal", in *Qualitative Research in Psychology*, Vol 1:1 pp 69–92

If I get pregnant, can anyone else decide whether I go ahead with it or not?

Chavez-Garcia, M. (2012) *States of Delinquency: Race and Science in the Making of California's Juvenile Justice System*. Oakland, California: University of California Press.

Haddad, L. B., & Nour, N. M. (2009). Unsafe Abortion: Unnecessary Maternal Mortality. *Reviews in Obstetrics and Gynecology*, 2:2, pp122–126.

Kaplan, Laura (1995) *The Story of Jane*. New York: Pantheon Books.

Sherwin, S. (1991). Abortion Through a Feminist Ethics Lens. *Dialogue*, 30:3, pp327–342. doi:10.1017/S0012217300011690

Stern, A. M. (2005). STERILIZED in the Name of Public Health: Race, Immigration, and Reproductive Control in Modern California. *American Journal of Public Health*, 95:7, pp1128–1138. http://doi.org/10.2105/AJPH.2004.041608

Why am I afraid to walk down the street?

Brownmiller, Susan (1975) *Against Our Will: Men, Women and Rape*. New York, NY: Simon and Schuster

MacKinnon, C. (1982) *Feminism Unmodified: discourses on life and law*. Cambridge, Mass: University of Harvard Press.

Rich, Adrienne. (1977). *Of Woman Born*. London: Virago.

Russell, D. E. (1982). "The prevalence and incidence of forcible rape and attempted rape of females." *Victimology*, 7:1-4, pp81–93.

Walby, Sylvia. (1990). *Theorizing patriarchy*. Oxford, UK: B. Blackwell.

Index

A

abortion 176–80
Adichie, Chimamanda Ngozi 14
advertising 146–7, 148, 172
agentic behaviours 115
Akhtar, Farhan 152
Alyokhina, Mariya 23
ambivalent sexism 28–31
ancient civilizations 121–2, 129–30
angel in the house 103–4
Angelou, Maya 144
Anthony, Susan B. 21
Aptheker, Bettina 33
Aristotle 10, 11, 116, 169
art world 128–9

B

Babcock, Linda 107–8
babies 96
backlash, anti-feminist 36, 37, 38–9
Bailey, Emma 175
Barkley Brown, Elsa 33
Barrios de Chungara, Domitila 15–16, 17
beauty myth 162–6
Beauvoir, Simone de 11, 13, 24, 31, 175
  and abortion 180
  on childhood 96–7
  and consumer culture 147
  on marriage 73, 75
  on motherhood 94
  The Second Sex 10, 12, 43, 56, 67, 68, 69
Bechdel Test 151
benevolent sexism 30–1, 43, 104, 107
Berdahl, Jennifer 127
Berger, John 139
Besant, Annie 178
Bigelow, Kathryn 149
biological essentialism 97
birdcage of sexism 24–6, 185
black and ethnic minority women 32, 33–5, 136, 144
  Kitchen Table Press 153–5
Blanch, Harriot Stanton 21
Boden, Alison 168
body shaming 14
Bonderman, David 26
Brady, Judy 81
Brazilian waxes 171, 174
Bronstein, Carolyn 174
Brontë, Charlotte 104–5
Brownmiller, Susan 183–5
Brush, Steven 131
Bullock, Sandra 152
Bunch, Charlotte 18
burkinis 122
Butler, Judith 69, 142–4

C

Cady Stanton, Elizabeth 11, 21, 22, 23
Cameron, David 26
caring professions 110
Carter, Angela 170
Cato the Elder 29
Cavalli Bastos, Cibelle 158
celebrities 137–40
Chesler, Phyllis 116
Chien-Shiung Wu 131
child sexual abuse 182
childcare 92–5, 107, 179–80
children
  choosing not to have 84–7
  gender roles 13, 96–9
  and pornography 174–5
Christianity and women's bodies 167–8
class 14, 33–5, 64–5, 182–3
Clements, Kirstie 162
Cleopatra 130
Cleyre, Voltairine 38
Clinton, Hillary 114, 123
clothes 39, 145, 168–9
  dress codes 120–3
colonialism 28
Combahee River Collective 35
compliments 31
consumer culture 145–7
contraception 177, 178, 179
Cornell, Drucilla 174
Crenshaw, Kimberlé 33
Criado-Perez, Caroline 96
cultural appropriation 148
Curie, Marie 130
cyberfeminists 135–6, 157–8

D

Daly, Mary 53
dating, paying for a date 42–4
Davis, Angela 35
Davis, Geena 151–2
Davison, Emily 20
Delaney, Janice 169
Dines, Gail 174
Diniz, Francisca 11
domesticity 102–5, 165
dress codes 120–3
Dworkin, Andrea 51, 64, 174, 182
dyadic dependent relationships 29, 31

E

Eagly, Alice 115
education of women 117–18
Edwards, Emily 162, 163
emotional, women as 116–18
Engels, Friedrich 59, 86
Enlightenment 117
equality 35, 36–9

F

fallen women 103
Faludi, Susan 36, 39
families 88–90
fashion industry 147–8
Fawcett, Millicent 20
femininity 10, 14, 162, 163–4
Ferguson, Ann 110
FGM (female genital mutilation) 16, 18, 54
Fifty Shades of Grey (James) 74
film, women in 149–52
Fine, Cordelia 98–9
Firestone, Shulamith 46, 47, 48, 52, 53, 59–60
  on the family 89
  on marriage proposals 66–7
  on motherhood 86–7, 95
  on women and paid work 109–10
first-wave feminists 11–12, 20, 109
Fiske, Mary 28–9, 30–1
Fletcher, Beryl 135
Fonda, Jane 156
four waves of feminism 11–14, 36
Fourier, Charles 18
France 23, 122–3, 180
Freedman, Estelle 11, 19, 177–8
freedom of expression 35
Freind, John 169–70
Freud, Sigmund 48, 55, 86, 170
Friedan, Betty 56–7, 78–9, 165
  The Feminine Mystique 81–3, 102–3, 145–6, 148
Friedman, Marilyn 75
Frye, Marilyn 24–6, 27, 185

G

gay liberation 88
gay marriage 66–7
Gay, Roxane 74, 75, 150
Geist, Claudia 125
gender fluidity 10
gender stereotypes 48, 62, 110
  ambivalent sexism 28–31
  dress codes 123
  in the workplace 113–15, 125
Gilbert, Sandra 104
Gillard, Julia 27
girl squad pictures 139–40
Glick, Peter 28–9, 30–1
goddess worship 167
Godwin, William 37
Gokova, Jonah 31
Gouges, Olympe de 11, 117
Gourion, Sophie 27
Greer, Germaine 55–6, 58–9, 68–9, 83
  on the family 89
  The Female Eunuch 84, 89
Gubar, Susan 104
Guerilla Girls 128–9, 130

Index

Acknowledgments

Tabi Jackon Gee: My rockstar of a Grandma Connie is the absolute number one dedicatee of this book (she once worked for Spare Rib) – but coming in at a very close joint second are dear friend Romilly Morgan and my mum Susie who both provide never-ending inspiration. Thanks also to the team at Octopus for a super introduction to writing books and to my co-author for helping me keep my cool.

Freya Rose: This book is for F and C – a plethora of life lessons! Huge thanks to my inspirational co-author and the great team at Octopus, especially illustrators Grace Helmer, Claire Huntley and Gareth Southwell, expert editor Ellie Corbett, and publisher Trevor Davies (who has always been one of the world's good guys).